Alfred Trumble

The Mysteries of Mormonism

A Full Exposure of it's Secret Practices and Hidden Crimes

Alfred Trumble

The Mysteries of Mormonism
A Full Exposure of it's Secret Practices and Hidden Crimes

ISBN/EAN: 9783743435568

Printed in Europe, USA, Canada, Australia, Japan

Cover: Foto ©Lupo / pixelio.de

More available books at **www.hansebooks.com**

THE
MYSTERIES
—OF—

A FULL EXPOSURE

OF

ITS SECRET PRACTICES AND HIDDEN CRIMES.

BY AN APOSTLE'S WIFE.

FULLY ILLUSTRATED.

PUBLISHED BY

RICHARD K. FOX, PROPRIETOR POLICE GAZETTE,
FRANKLIN SQUARE, NEW YORK.

Entered according to Act of Congress, in the year 1881, by
RICHARD K. FOX,
Publisher of the POLICE GAZETTE,
NEW YORK,
In the Office of the Librarian of Congress, at Washington.

CONTENTS.

CHAPTER.	PAGE.
I.—THE "DESTROYING ANGELS" FOILED.	7
II.—THE ORIGIN OF MORMONISM,	10
III.—THE MORMON GOSPEL,	13
IV.—MORMON POLYGAMY AND GOVERNMENT.	16
V.—MORMON MIRACLES,	20
VI.—JOE SMITH MOVES WEST,	25
VII.—BRIGHAM YOUNG STEPS IN,	28
VIII.—THE CRIMES OF MORMONISM,	33
IX.—THE DANITES,	36
X.—SECRETS OF THE ENDOWMENT HOUSE,	42
XI.—MORMON WIVES,	52
XII.—MEN WITH MANY WIVES,	59
XIII.—A MORMON WIFE'S STORY,	68
XIV.—THE DOOM OF MORMONISM,	87

IN THE HOLY BATH.

THE MYSTERIES OF MORMONISM.

CHAPTER I.

THE "DESTROYING ANGELS" FOILED.

Mormonism has well been called the twin relic of barbarism. It is more. It is an infamy even modern barbarism scarcely tolerates. The Turk preserves a certain decency in the public management of his seraglio nowadays, and the Orientally audacious flaunting of his sensual indulgence which makes the old romances of the East so unique in their naughty piquancy has vanished. He has his scores of wives still but he keeps them in private, and when he goes among men who are not of his faith he does not attempt to proselytize them or to extend his branded creed.

How different it is with the devotee of that bestial belief who covers, or essays to cover, the rottenness of his creed with the claim to Divine endorsement, thanks to which he dubs himself a Latter Day Saint!

No modest obscurity for him! No humble enjoyment of his licentious worships in the secrecy of his own house! The world must know it; and not only that, the world must contribute to its support and expansion. The Mormon missionary goes abroad in the highways and byways of the earth, preaching his creed of the bagnio to the ignorant and depraved and gathering them into the fold.

If Mormonism had its root in the remote wilds of Siberia this condition of affairs would be bad enough. What can be said of it, then, when it nestles in the bosom of the greatest and freest nation of the earth and blots the boasted civilization of a republic which has done more in a century than any other governments in all their existences to enlighten and improve the world?

The polygamy of the Mormon community is the foulest ulcer on the body of our nation. The trial of the assassin of President Gar-

EVERY WIFE IS GIVEN SO MUCH OF THE HUSBAND'S MONEY.

years she was a wanderer, pursued by phantom foes whose implacability was on a par with their persistency. Twice in France, once in England and thrice in the United States, was she compelled to call upon the strong arm of the law to shield her, and each time the same mysterious threat of ultimate destruction was conveyed to her from an enemy who might be baffled but not defeated.

At last accident came to her rescue.

Last year a passenger steamer on its way from Europe to America was wrecked and many lives were lost. The passenger list was published. Among the names upon it was the writer's and it belonged to one of the drowned.

That name was entered in the "red book," the sinister record kept of the foes whom Mormonism has denounced. Against it was set a black cross and the remark, "The Lord hath conquered! Glory to his name!"

Thus, dead but alive, I give this work to the world. It was written during years of wandering, and chapters of it first saw the light in many foreign lands. But it is complete and honest. What it may lack in style it makes up in fact. It is no fault of mine that the stories it tells read like romances and are a shame upon the land in which their incidents were enacted.

I trust and desire that the reader will remember this.

I write from actual experience. I tell nothing I am not aware of the truth of; there is not one of the romantic events, the shocking crimes and the infamous observances I tell of which has not every foundation of its occurrence for existence here.

I make these revelations in the interest of society and of the world. I hope my pages will be a warning to some who are rashly about to enter on the gloomy and debased path I have followed to my sorrow; I trust they will encourage by my example some who have entered into the shadow of shame to withdraw while there is yet time.

So much for myself; now for my work.

CHAPTER II.

THE ORIGIN OF MORMONISM.

Mormonism was a swindle from the very start. It is to-day a monstrous crime grown from the successful fraud of a shrewd confidence operator.

The founder of Mormonism was Joseph Smith. Born at Sharon, Windsor County, Vermont, on Dec. 23, 1805, he came of the worst of a bad breed. His parents were "hard cases," and renowned as such throughout the neighborhood. When, in 1815, they removed to Palmyra, Wayne County, N. Y., there was an universal expression of satisfaction on all sides.

The Smiths recommenced in New York their existence in Vermont. They avoided honest labor and lived on credit, not without suspicion of having more than a passing knowledge of their neighbors' fields and henroosts. Nowadays they would have probably become tramps. Then they were tolerated because people did not know how to get rid of them.

There was only one business the Smiths indulged in with any show of industry. When they were sober enough (for they were lusty topers) they were perpetually digging for buried treasure. Next to this pursuit they starred in the nefarious one of sheep stealing. In 1833 upwards of sixty leading citizens of Wayne County, who were called upon to depose as to the character of the Smiths, testified under oath that they were immoral, false and fraudulent, and that the hopeful Joseph was the worse of the lot.

Yet this is the man who founded what he dared call a faith, and grafted on the United States the religion of licentiousness and bodily lust known as Mormonism.

What a clever, bright, intelligent man this must have been, though, says the reader. On the contrary; he was an ignorant, brutal loafer. He could scarcely read, wrote a hand scarcely anyone, even himself, could understand, and was ignorant even of the elementary rules of arithmetic. But he was shrewd, fearless and inventive. Living among a country community where superstitions were commonly current, he

MOBBING A MORMON MEETING.

MORMON RITES.

had wit enough to comprehend the value of superstition as a means of defrauding its votaries. He began active life by wandering about the country with a divining rod, seeking water and buried treasure. Then, finding that religious ideas of a novel sort were popular just then, he turned his attention in that direction.

According to his own report he commenced to have visions at the age of fifteen, when, on Sept. 21, 1823, the angel Moroni appeared to him three times, instructing him that God had selected him for the prophet of the new and real faith. According to this account the angel sent Smith to a hill in Manchester, Ontario County, N. Y., to dig up the record of the faith, written on plates of gold, and a sort of celestial spectacles made of two transparent stones, without which it would be impossible for him to peruse the auriferous chronicles.

No one ever saw either the golden plates or the spectacles. The former were described as being eight inches long, seven inches wide, about as thick as stout tin foil, and bound together by three rings. The latter Smith gave the fantastic name of Urium and Thummerum, and said they were presented to him by the angel Moroni on Sept. 22, 1822.

With the aid of these spectacles Joseph Smith, sitting behind a blanket to preserve the precious records from profane eyes, claimed to read off the "Golden Bible," as he called it, to one Oliver Cowdery, who wrote it down as he heard it. The account thus dictated claimed to be a history of the prehistoric inhabitants of America, and of the dealings of God with them on the basis of a true faith.

Such is the origin of Mormonism, according to the Mormons. Now for the facts:

About 1740, there was born in Ashford, Conn., one Solomon Spaulding. He graduated at Dartmouth College and was ordained for the ministry in 1761. He soon tired of preaching, and about four years later became a store keeper at Cherry Valley, N. Y., whence, in 1809, he removed to Conneaut, Ohio, the scene, by-the-bye, of a recent prize fight of some notoriety. In 1812, Spaulding removed to Pittsburg, Pa., and in 1814 to Amity, where he died in 1816.

This wandering backslider from the ministry was a visionary with a marked turn for literature. He wrote novels of such a worthless character that he could never get them published, so they perished in manuscript, after having been read by his friends. While he was living in Ohio he wrote a romance to account for the peopling of America by deriving the Indians from the Jews. It was an absurd book, which to-day would probably not find a single reader.

The writer of it gave it out as a manuscript found in an Indian mound or cave in Ohio. He called it "Manuscript Found," and one of its sections was called the "Book of Mormon." All these facts were publicly known ten years before Joseph Smith turned up with his new religion.

In order to understand how Smith got hold of them I must introduce a new character.

Sidney Rigdon was born in St. Clair Township, Allegheny County, Pa., on Feb. 19, 1793. In 1812 Rigdon, who had learned the printing trade, was connected with a printing office at Pittsburg. To this place Solomon Spaulding brought his "Manuscript Found" to have it put into book form. It was not printed then, but Rigdon, who found it lying about the office, became possessed of an idea that he could use it at some time, so he copied it. The original manuscript was returned to the author, "declined with thanks," as many other manuscripts have been before and since. The copy Sidney Rigdon kept for himself.

Soon after this Rigdon gave up type-setting and set out to preach his way to fortune and fame. New religions were in fashion in those days, and he had one which included many ideas from Solomon Spaulding's manuscript and other original ones which are now found in the Mormon creed.

In 1829 he fell in with Joseph Smith. Smith had already made a start with his new religion, but he had no ideas to back it. He had told the story of the golden plates, but endeavored to make no explanation of what was inscribed on them. Rigdon saw the value of a combination of ideas in this matter and lost no time in effecting it. He formed a partnership with Smith and read to him the romance of Solomon Spaulding.

It must be remembered that Spaulding did not pretend that his "Book of Mormon" or the "Manuscript Found," of which it was a portion, was anything but a dime novel. But Rigdon and Smith set it up for holy writ, and compared it with the tablets of stone on which God's commandments were written for the observance of Moses and his people.

It was this intention of Spaulding's with variations, that Joseph

BIDDING FOR A WIFE.

HOW THEY DO IT AND THEN RUE IT.

Smith dictated to Oliver Cowdery from behind the blankets. It was printed in 1830, in a book of some 300 pages, along with a statement by three witnesses, Cowdery, David Whitmer and Martin Harris, that they had seen an angel bring the golden plates from Heaven. Harris was a farmer who advanced the money to print the book. These worthies afterwards had a falling out, and acknowledged that their statement was a lie, and that all they knew of the plates was what Smith had told them.

However, Smith and Rigdon were well fixed for work with their bogus bible. As soon as they had it complete they began to preach its tenets. It will interest the reader to be briefly informed what these were.

CHAPTER III.

THE MORMON GOSPEL.

The "Book of Mormon" consists of sixteen books, professing to be written by as many different prophets. In it over three hundred passages of the Christian Bible are found, stolen without credit. Names of Hebrew, Greek and Latin origin are used in it indiscriminately.

According to it, one Lehi dwelt in Jerusalem with his family in the days of King Zedekiah, six hundred years B. C. The Lord sent him into the wilderness of Arabia where he dwelt for a long time. Then he got another divine command and set out on a journey for eight years, which landed them on the sea shore. There they built a ship and sailed for America. They landed on the coast of Chili. The emigrants consisted of Lehi, his wife, his four sons, Laman, Lemuel, Sam and Nephi, their four wives, two "sons of Ishmael" and their two wives, and Zoram, a servant and his wife, eight grown men in all and as many women. There were also two infant sons of Lehi, born in the journey. Their names were Jacob and Joseph.

Lehi died soon after his arrival in America, and his sons had a row and split up. Nephi and his younger brother Sam, with the servant, Zoram, and their families and Jacob and Joseph, moved into the wilderness, with some followers. The rest God cursed till their skin grew red and they became Indians. Such, according to Joseph Smith,

Sidney Rigdon **and Solomon** Spaulding was the **commencement of the history** of America. **Nephi** started this history, **and in** his time the race increased **and multiplied** very fast. After **his** death his descendants succeeded **him in power,** and waxed **rich and strong.**

Finally **came one, Nephi the second, and** during his rule an awful earthquake **announced the** crucifixion. **Three** days after, Christ himself appeared **out of heaven, showed the Nephites** his wounds, taught **them,** performed **miracles and so on for forty days,** leaving them possessed of **the same Christianity as that of the** Bible, **from** which Spaulding, Rigdon **and Smith** had paraphrased **their** dime novel, Holy Writ. **All this while, however, the** Nephites and their dusky brethren, **the** Indians, were **at war, and finally, in a great** battle **on the hill of** Cumorah, in Western New **York,** A. D., **384, the** Christian Nephites were **nearly** annihilated.

The records **of** the race, which **had** been **written on the** plates of gold by a prophet named Moroni, were buried in this hill nearly forty years later (A. D., 420) by Moroni, who had survived the **battle** in order **to** become an angel and appear to **Joseph** Smith in 1823, and tell him where **to** dig **in order** to find and re-establish the buried faith. Such, in brief, and in much more reasonable language, **is** the cheerful fiction on **which the Mormon** faith is based : **a sort** of garbled Bible, well mixed **with the fantastic** romance **of the** vagabond Yankee **preacher** who, having **started by** writing dull **and innocent** novels **which nobody** would read, **ended by unintentionally establishing a religion of lust** which is an outrage **on the civilized world.**

As for the religion Joe Smith **and his** fellow sharpers **built** out of this **romance, it is as** fantastic **as the cause they** offer for its existence itself. **They believe in a God, who was** once a man, and grew too **pure and** good **for earth, so was made ruler of** all mankind. This God, they hold, **was married in due form to the** Virgin Mary by the angel Gabriel. **Christ was the** offspring **of the** union. For the rest, it would puzzle a **conjuror to** make clear head or tail of the Mormon doctrines, except that Joe Smith was a god on earth, and that any man by imitating his example in purity and holiness can become deity himself.

But the easiest **way to** show the Mormon doctrines up to contempt **is to** let them **explain** themselves. The following are the articles of **faith ;**

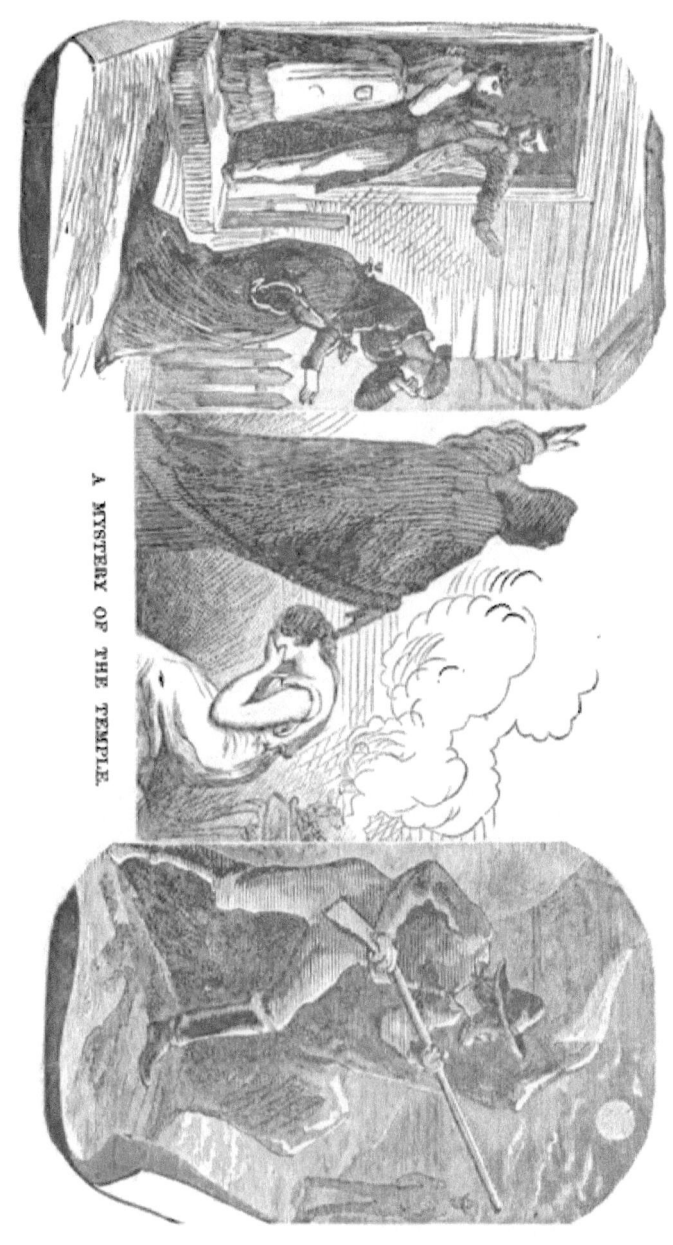

A MYSTERY OF THE TEMPLE.

TEMPLE MUMMERIES.

1. "We believe in God, the Eternal Father, and his son, Jesus Christ, and in the Holy Ghost.

2. "We believe that men will be punished for their own sins, and not for Adam's transgressions.

3. "We believe that through the Atonement of Christ all mankind may be saved by obedience to the laws and ordinances of the Gospel.

4. "We believe these ordinances are, 1st, Faith in the Lord Jesus; 2d, Repentence; 3d, Baptism by immersion for the remission of sins; 4th, Laying on of hands by the gift of the Holy Spirit; 5th, the 'Lord's Supper.'

5. "We believe that man must be called of God by inspiration, and by laying on of hands from those who are duly commissioned to preach the Gospel and administer in the ordinances thereof.

6. "We believe in the same organization that existed in the primitive Church, viz.: Apostles, Prophets, Pastors, Evangelists, etc.

7. "We believe in the powers and gifts of the everlasting Gospel, viz.: the Gift of Faith, discerning of Spirits, prophecy, revelations, visions, healing, tongues, and the interpretation of tongues, wisdom, charity, brotherly love, etc.

8. "We believe the word of God recorded in the Bible; we also believe the Word of God recorded in the Book of Mormon, and in all other good books.

9. "We believe all that God has revealed, all that he does now reveal, and we believe that he will reveal many more great and important things pertaining to the Kingdom of God and Messiah's second coming.

10. "We believe in the literal gathering of Israel and in the restoration of the Ten Tribes; that Zion will be established upon the Western Continent, and that Christ will reign personally upon the earth for a thousand years; and that the earth will be renewed and receive its paradisiacal glory.

11. "We believe in the literal resurrection of the body, and that the rest of the dead live not again until the thousand years are expired.

12. "We claim the privilege of worshipping Almighty God according to the dictates of conscience unmolested, and allow all men the same privilege, let them worship how or when they may.

13. "We believe in being subject to Kings, Queens, Presidents,

Rulers and Magistrates, in obeying, honoring and sustaining the law.

14. "We believe in being honest, true, chaste, temperate, benevolent, virtuous and upright, and in doing good to all men; indeed, we may say that we follow the admonition of Paul; we believe all things, we hope all things, we have endured very many things and hope to be able to endure all things. Everything lovely, virtuous, praiseworthy, and of good report, we seek after, looking forward to he recompense of reward; but an idle or lazy person cannot be a Christian, neither have salvation. He is a drone, and destined to be stung to death, and tumbled out of the hive."

CHAPTER IV.

MORMON POLYGAMY AND GOVERNMENT.

It will doubtless surprise many of my readers to learn that polygamy has no foundation either in the principal of faith promulgated by Joseph Smith and the founders of the Mormon gospel. Polygamy not only fails to receive their sanction but the "Book of Mormon" and the "Book of Doctrine and Covenants" condemn the practice in the most emphatic language.

The sentiment of the Book of Mormon upon the subject of polygamy can be understood from the following quotation, page 116:

"Behold David and Solomon truly had many wives and concubines, which thing was abominable before me, saith the Lord, wherefore I have led this people forth out of the land of Jerusalem by the power of mine arm, that I might raise up unto me a righteous branch from the fruit of the loins of Joseph. Wherefore I, the Lord, will not suffer that this people shall do like unto them of old; wherefore, my brethren, hear me, and hearken unto the word of the Lord. For there shall not any man among you have save it be one wife, and concubines he shall have none."

We see from this quotation that polygamy is not only prohibited, but the example of the old patriarchs, which the polygamist sets so much store by, flinging it in the face of the decent people of this land as an excuse for his crime against the laws of God and man, is here declared to have been an abomination.

How, then, asks the reader, did polygamy originate? I answer,

"MANY TIMES HE STRUCK ME DOWN WITH HIS FIST."

SHE WAS TYRANNICAL.

it was born in the foul and lustful brain of Brigham Young and was grafted on the faith to gratify his sensual bestiality.

In August, 1852, Brigham Young produced a document before a conference of the Utah church, which he claimed was a revelation given to Joseph Smith in July, 1843, commanding the church to enter into polygamy. No explanation was given for keeping it concealed for nine years except that it was nobody's business. This paper was not in the handwriting of Joseph Smith as all similar ones received by the church had been. To account for this fatal defect Brigham stated that "Sister Emma," the wife of Joseph Smith, had thrown the original in the fire.

This story was pronounced a fabrication by Emma Smith, who testified just before her death that she had never seen or heard of any such revelation until Brigham Young brought it forward in 1852. But there are other evidences going to show that this precious document is a forgery. This pretended revelation is dated July 12, 1843. In it polygamy is commanded under pain of eternal damnation, but on Feb. 1, 1844, we have a notice published in the "Times and Seasons" that one "Hiram Brown had been cut off from the church for teaching polygamy and other false and corrupt doctrines."

This is signed by Joseph and Hiram Smith; that is to say, the man who, according to Brigham Young, commanded his followers to embrace polygamy as a portion of their creed, a year after the promulgation of this command punished one of his followers for doing what it commanded.

Brigham Young was no fanatic in religion. Like the great Napoleon he was ambitious of creating an empire of which he should be the head. To gain such power as he desired and to gather adherents around him he offered men such inducements as have not been within their legitimate grasp since the old Biblical days, that is, among Europeans. How greedily the bait was swallowed is now matter of history. Having once founded his dynasty he knew how to render it solid. He never allowed laboring men to be idle. If there was no work to do he would create it. I have known him to set men digging a canal in order to keep them employed, and when it was dug he would order them to fill it.

Brig., as he came familiarly to be called by the faithful, was as wise as ever Napoleon was. He believed that wealth, even more than knowledge, was power and he allowed no man to become too rich and thus threaten his place. As soon as a man began to be wealthy it was cunningly suggested to him that he ought to take another wife, and another, and another, so as to keep his means down to a certain point, and no one could rise to any exalted position in the church unless he was a polygamist, for there are numbers of Mormons who are no polygamists.

Thus, then, polygamy was invented by Brigham Young partially to gratify his own lustful instincts and partly to prevent any of his followers from becoming opulent enough to be independent of him and his commands.

In the Mormon church there are almost as great a variety and number of officials as it takes to run a political party. But for all this it is a greater despotism than the government of Russia.

The head of the church is imperial master over all Mormonism and all Mormons. The lives and property of his followers are at his command and they bow in slavish subjection before him. Although they profess to pray to a God they really pray to him as the purest of beings alive, next to God himself in virtue and beneficence.

Still he is nominally only one of several chieftains, as the following explanation of the government of the Mormon church will explain. The chief officers of the church are:

The Presidency.—This consists of three individuals, the third president being also Mayor of Salt Lake City, Secretary of State of the State of Deseret, and Lieutenant-General of the militia of the Territory. They are known respectively as the 1st, 2d and 3d presidents and constitute the supreme power among the Mormons in all matters. Brigham Young was the great power that controlled the presidency in the recent past. The presidents are elected by the people, the masses of whom regard the first president as unsurpassed in wisdom save by God himself. A simple expression of his wishes is undisputed authority and is obeyed implicitly.

II. *The Patriarch.*—This official's duties consist in bestowing patriarchal blessings upon the faithful who desire them and are willing to pay for them. He will lay his reverend hands upon the head of a saint and bless him with houses and lands and wives (number specified) and children and heirship to eternal glory, if faithful. These blessings are written out and signed by the patriarch and are highly prized by the ignorant.

III. *The Twelve Apostles.*—Or, as they style themselves, "Special witnesses of the name of Christ in all the world." This body ranks next after the presidency. The apostles ordain subordinate clerical officials, baptize, administer the sacrament, supervise missionary labor and are the chief preachers and expounders of the faith.

IV. *The Seventy.*—Are the missionaries out of the first seventy appointed. Seven were elected presidents, and these appointed other seventies, who also had presidents and appointed others, so that, by a species of exaggerated compound interest the number of missionaries keeps constantly increasing. The missionaries are supposed to pay all their own expenses, but they don't.

V. *The High Priest.*—These are church officials, elected principally to do the first president's dirty work, as they can officiate in any office he chooses to appoint them to when he wants his will carried out.

VI. *The Bishops.*—Although they bear an ecclesiastical title, are really rather temporal officials. There is one appointed to every Mormon settlement, and one to every ward in Salt Lake City. They are collectors of tithes, keep the census of their several districts, and settle difficulties existing among the saints, when they can do so, subject to appeal to higher authority. They are supposed to administer to the spiritual wants of the people of their charge, and visit their homes for this purpose. In Salt Lake City there is a chief Bishop, and he is the channel through which any matter of business the Ward Bishop may be unable to settle to the satisfaction of the parties, or any grievance, must be communicated to higher authority, that is to say, the First President.

VII. *The High Council.*—This consists of twelve High Priests, with the President of the Church at its head. It is the highest authority to which parties may appeal when they feel aggrieved by the decision of their Bishop or other local authority. The President is required to give the decision in all cases brought before the Council when the others vote upon it.

The reader may imagine how far the opinion of one who is thought incapable to err has to do with the vote of the Council. Its jurisdiction is confined to temporal matters.

Besides the officials of the church here enumerated there are several other classes knows as elders, priests, teachers, and deacons. but as the duties of all these are included among those of higher grades, and as they interlace and overlap each other, so I will not occupy more space in referring to them.

This, in brief, is the Mormon scheme of Government. No matter who you are, or how serious or trivial your business may be, it is subject to the authority of the Bishops, who are, in effect, but figureheads who act through higher deputies for the First President himself. You cannot escape him, for his is the hand which governs the machine in which you are shut up to furnish the motive power as fire and water are held imprisoned to keep an engine going.

In the pages which follow the workings of this detestable system will be made clearer by example. My purpose in explaining the Mormon hierarchy here is to simplify a comprehension of what is to come.

We have now learned the origin of Mormonism, its principles and its method of enforcing and sustaining them. Now let us see how the loathsome weed grew into a a rank Upas tree whose shade cast moral death over one of the fairest sections of the continent.

CHAPTER V.

MORMON MIRACLES.

The first issue of the Gospel of Mormon was published, as we have said, in 1820. The book dictated by Joseph Smith, with the help of Sidney Rigdon and Solomon Spaulding, written by Oliver Cowdery and published with farmer Harris' money, soon attracted attention. It hit the taste of the time. The villages of western New York were just then in a ferment over new religions of all sorts, and the inventors of Mormonism had cunningly contrived their work so as to please the many. When Smith went about preaching his new gospel he found many followers, and as these joined the ranks they were made active agents to extend the faith too, just as the "Seventies" are increased now.

Missionaries were sent out all around to proclaim the new gospel. As evidence of their divine authority they pretended to work miracles. Early in its history the new sect was subjected to rigid persecution.

ARRIVAL OF AN INSTALLMENT OF WIVES AT SALT LAKE.

Its meetings were mobbed, the members stoned and some even killed. This only increased their fanaticism, and Joseph Smith soon entertained the idea of establishing a temporal sovereignty.

An excellent example of the means Smith used to make converts is given in the following description of a "miracle," performed in New York State before a woman whom the prophet wanted to convert. The story was told by her to me, years afterwards, and I give it in her own language as I then wrote it down:

"The room in which the Mormons were assembled was a large oblong hall, with curtained windows. The furniture consisted of a few rude benches, and a table resembling a huge desk stood at the upper end, on which a small candle was feebly burning. It was impossible to form anything like a correct calculation of the numbers assembled, on account of the obscurity. I could only perceive an indiscriminate mixture of men and women, many of whom were fantastically disguised. Some were seated, others standing; but the High Priest of the ceremonies had not yet arrived.

"Smith came in immediately. He was a tall, graceful-looking man, not handsome, but of imposing appearance. He wore black, had dark, piercing eyes, and though he did not look like a gentleman, did not look like the sheep-stealing vagabond I had known him for a few years before, either.

"A murmur of admiration greeted his entrance, and he smiled at it as if conscious of his power.

"He commenced to speak and the utmost silence prevailed. His discourse was on the nature of miracles. I observed that he quoted more from the scriptures than the Mormon bible. The sermon was very short, in order that more time might be employed in the performance of miracles.

"At its close the light was removed from the desk and placed in a socket directly over it. Smith then knelt; the others followed his example, and the whole company remained some time in silent prayer. At length he rose; the others still knelt. After a moment's silence he uttered the solemn and impressive words:

"'It is my word, saith the Lord, ye shall be delivered from death, which is the power of the devil, from sorrow and sighing. Therefore, in the might of the Spirit, I command you, bring forth your dead!'

"The deep stillness which succeeded these words was awfully impressive. The door slowly opened, and two men entered bearing a corpse. It was the body of a young and beautiful female, clad in the white habiliments of death, and looking, Oh! how ghastly and ghostly in the dim obscurity of the uncertain light. The limbs were stiff and rigid, the eyes and mouth partially open, and the whole aspect of the countenance that of death. The bearers stretched her on the desk. Smith turned to them with an expression of feature I could not fathom; Ward stood beside him, and I detected him glancing more than once at myself.

"'Whose child is this?' said Smith.

"'Mine,' answered one of the men, solemnly.

"'Did she die suddenly?'

"'She did.'

"'When?'

"'This afternoon.'

"'Believest thou?'

"'I believe,' said the man, impressively, 'help thou my unbelief.'

"'Did this child believe?'

"'She was a believer.'

"''Tis well; thy child shall be restored.'

"There was a faint shriek from the group of spectators, and a woman, whom I subsequently ascertained to be the mother of the dead, rushed forward and threw herself at the feet of Smith.

"'Restore my child,' she cried, passionately; 'she was too young, too good, and too beautiful to die. Restore her, and I will worship you for ever.'

"'Woman, I said it,' he replied; then turning to the company he said, 'let some one of the sisters look after this woman, she must not be permitted to interfere.'

"Mrs. Bradish went forward, and raising the woman, led her to a seat.

"'Let the believers rise,' resumed Smith, 'and sing the Hallelujah Chant.'

"A moment after the strain begun, low at first, but swelling out wild and tumultuous as the enthusiasm increased, and the passions of the assembly were brought into exercise:

"'When Nephi came out of Palestine,
 and Tebi from among the heathen,

The great and mighty ocean was driven back before them;
The mountains fled away;
The hills sank in the lakes;
And the rivers were dried up.
There was life brought back from death,
And souls restored from the grave,
By the mighty power of faith.
 Hallelujah!
And it shall be so again,
 Hallelujah!
Even now our eyes behold it,
 Hallelujah!
The pale, cold corpse is waking,
 Hallelujah!
Strength is returning to its limbs,
 Hallelujah!
We shall see her again as we have seen her
 Hallelujah!
In the pride and beauty of life,
 Hallelujah!
With no cerements clinging to her bosom,
 Hallelujah!
It comes, the power of the Most High God forever,
 Hallelujah!
He has listened to the voice of His servant and apostle,
 Hallelujah!
He has arrested the might of death at His bidding,
 Hallelujah!
As He did at the bidding of Moses and Elijah,
 Hallelujah!
As He did at the bidding of Christ and Saul of Tarsus,
 Hallelujah!'

"As the chant went on voice after voice tired out and ceased, til the whole ended in profound silence. Smith meanwhile stood be- e the apparently dead body. He pressed and stroked the head, athed into the mouth and rubbed the frigid limbs, saying in a low, ip voice:

"'Live thou again, young woman. Let sight return to these eyes, now sightless, and strength to these limbs, now nerveless. Let life and vigor and animation inspire this wasted frame.'

"Presently there was a slight movement of the muscles, the eyes opened and shut, the arms were flung out and then brought together again; and at last the body sat up. The effect on the assembly was electrical. The mother fell into violent hysterics; many of the females shrieked, others sobbed.

"I stood gazing, absorbed, almost incapable of sense or motion; my reasoning faculties altogether at fault on such a subject. A voice breathed in my ear:

"'Dost thou now believe?'

"I turned; Mr. Ward was at my side.

"'I am astonished, if not convinced.'

"'You have seen the dead restored to life. Look; she speaks and walks.'

"I looked, it was indeed as he said. She had descended from the table, and with her grave clothes on, was making the circuit of the room, leaning on the arm of Smith. Her cheeks were flushed with life and health, her eyes sparkled with animation, and her rounded and voluptuous form contrasted strangely with her ghastly habiliments."

This performance, I may as well explain here, was gotten up, as the witness afterwards found, exclusively for her benefit. The girl was no more dead than I am as I write. But these miracles were well worked and they made many converts. I remember another I once heard of, told me by an old lady who had witnessed it in Missouri where it occurred.

"There were two families by the name of Pulsifer, both believers in Mormon," she said. "A child died in one of these families, and the Mormons gave out that, on a certain night, an angel would come and carry the body to heaven. The time appointed arrived, the relatives of the dead were assembled, when a figure in white, and with small bells attached to its garments, appeared. A party of the unbelievers, lying in ambush, immediately gave chase. The figure ran for a neighboring swamp, but was pursued, taken, stripped of its angel robes, and proved to be Pulsifer, the uncle of the deceased."

Smith also used to throw people into trances, for he possessed a powerful degree of magnetic power. This not being understood by

HE HAD A CHOICE LOT.

DEVOUT MORMONS ON THEIR WAY TO THE TEMPLE, RAIN OR NO RAIN.

the ignorant and credulous masses among whom he practiced went for a divine gift, and invested him with tremendous and awful importance in their eyes.

CHAPTER VI.

JOE SMITH MOVES WEST.

By the beginning of 1831 Joe Smith had gathered quite a following, but his doctrines had many enemies, and he was so open and so savagely attacked that he concluded it prudent to move West. He settled on Kirtland, Ohio, as the scene of the New Jerusalem.

There they set up a bank, opened stores, and went on making new converts. Churches were soon established in Ohio, Pennsylvania, New York, Illinois, and still the eyes of the faith turned westward, to the great prairies where they hoped to be allowed to work out their system in peace and freedom. This led to the purchase by them of an extensive tract of land in Jackson County, Missouri, where another colony was set up.

In addition to the burning words of their missionaries, two newspapers were established, one a monthy, the *Morning and Evening Star*, and the other a weekly, the *Upper Missouri Advertiser*. Industry, energy, sobriety, order and cleanliness were the rules of the colonies. Polygamy was not thought of yet, and the new-made Mormons were enthusiastic and happy.

After Smith had established the colony in Missouri he returned to Kirkland and resumed work at converting new believers and perfecting the organization of his followers.

But here, as in New York, he had to submit to persecution and violence. Thus, on the night of March 22, 1832, a mob of Methodists, Baptists, Campbellites and other miscellaneous zealots broke into the prophet's house, tore him from his wife's arms, hurried him into an adjoining meadow and tarred and feathered him. Sidney Rigdon received similar treatment, and was rendered temporarily insane, but Smith preached next day, "his flesh all scarified and defaced," and proved the folly of persecution by baptizing three new converts that afternoon.

The Mormon leaders were not the only ones who came in for personal affliction at the hands of the enemy. Any man was liable to be set upon if he ventured far among the Gentiles, nor were the women spared. One was caught on a winter night, tied to a tree and buried under a mound of snow six feet high. And another was stripped naked and left to run a couple of miles over the icy roads to the nearest Mormon shelter. With such violences as these did the unbelievers force the followers of Smith into a closer and more stubborn adherence to their leader.

In Missouri the colony continued to prosper too, but secret societies were organized against it, its printing press was destroyed, and finally, in 1833, all hands were driven out of house and home, across the Missouri, and forced to camp in the wilderness on a bitter winter night. They rallied, however, and found a place to settle in Clay County. There they remained some three years.

It was here that Brigham Young was received into the church, and here in 1835, that he received his first office, being made one of the apostles.

Young was sent East to drum up converts among the Yankees, and such was his sagacity and force of character that he managed to make many proselytes even among this acute people. Two other famous apostles, Arson Hyde and Heber C. Kimball, were, in 1837, dispatched as missionaries to England, where they made hundreds of converts from the masses in the great commercial and manufacturing towns and among the laborers in the agricultural district.

All this gave Mormonism a great "boom," and Smith began to view the future with the eye of a conqueror. His hundreds of followers had swollen to thousands; his thousands of treasure to hundreds of thousands. Small parties of ruffians no longer attacked the Mormons. They had to fight in strong bands now, or run a strong chance of being thrashed themselves.

Such was the state of affairs when, at the end of 1837, the bank at Kirtland, Ohio, stopped payment. The State authorities at once took action against Joe Smith and a couple of his chief followers for swindling.

At this opportune moment the prophet received a "revelation." The reader will probably note by the time he gets through this book that Mormon leaders get revelations just at the right time.

This "revelation" commanded the prophet to move to Missouri,

THE MORMON EVE.

A YOUNG WIFE'S GLORY DAYS.

and thither the Ohio colony went to consolidate with the resident one, and he lost no time in obeying it.

The Missourians, however, were tireless in their attacks on the colonists. The truth was there were a good many hard cases among the Mormons, and these committed depredations on the property of the Gentile farmers which afforded the latter excellent excuse for retaliation. The result was that a sort of guerrilla warfare was kept up that began in time to assume the proportions of a veritable civil war.

In the course of these troubles Joe Smith was arrested by the State authorities, along with Sidney Rigdon, and locked up. He secured his release in 1838, and immediately had another "revelation." Thanks to this he moved all his followers, to the number of 15,000, across the river to Illinois, where at a spot some 220 miles above St. Louis, on a grant of land which they had obtained in the vicinity of the town of Commerce, they founded a city which a "revelation" told Smith to name Nauvoo, or the city of beauty.

The legislature of Illinois granted a charter to Nauvoo; a body of militia was formed under the name of the Nauvoo Legion, of which the prophet was named commander. He was also made mayor of the city and thus became actual as well as spiritual "boss."

When the Mormons settled at Nauvoo the land was a wilderness, but they soon had it blooming like a rose. A future of prosperity seemed before them, when trouble rose in a new quarter, or rather from a new cause.

This was a rumor that the Mormons, in addition to their queer doctrines of faith, were also practicing polygamy.

This was not really the fact. Rigdon had a theory about "spiritual wives" which Smith denounced for a long time, but ended by accepting. According to this theory women could only be saved through their husbands, and unmarried females must be ever debarred from the pleasures of the blest. Consequently every woman had to be provided with a spiritual husband, and as there were more women than men among the Mormons Rigdon and those who believed in him undertook to make the odd ones sure of heaven by marrying them himself. Smith was compelled to fall in with this idea in practice and the business of "sealing" extra wives was commenced.

Polygamy was not openly advocated, however. The spiritual wife was said to be united to her husband by a purely spiritual tie, independent of all sensual relations and was not supposed to have any carnal affinity with him whatever.

The unbelievers in Mormonism would not believe this, however, and serious disturbances broke out again.

In consequence of these Joe Smith, his brother Hiram and some of his chief supporters were arrested and thrown into prison at Carthage to await trial.

After a short time a rumor began to circulate to the effect that the Governor of the State desired to permit the two Smiths to escape. This news, true or false, was received with a veritable howl of fury. A mob of 200 men collected, armed to the teeth, on June 27, 1844. They marched to the prison, forced an entrance and swarmed in upon the prophet in his cell. The father of Mormonism fell, riddled with balls, and his brother was promptly sent to join him.

Thus, after 14 years of troublous existence, was Mormonism left without a head, in a world filled with furious and implacable enemies.

Thus did Joe Smith, sheep-stealer, treasure-hunter, wizard of the divining rod, having gulled and swindled his way to notoriety and power, go down the dark road by the same violence which, in the end, must sweep the loathsome faith he founded from the earth it soils.

CHAPTER VII.

BRIGHAM YOUNG STEPS IN.

We have already introduced the man who was destined to raise Mormonism to really vigorous power. Let us inquire a little more closely into his history. Brigham Young, however ignoble and detestable his work, was undoubtedly one of the most remarkable men in American history and deserves more than the brief notice we have given him in a book devoted to the cause whose most potent and sagacious champion he was.

Brigham Young was born at Whittingham, Vt., on June 1, 1801. He was the son of a man who owned and cultivated a little farm which afforded his family the barest and most miserable of livings.

After a youth of poverty, in the course of which he managed to secure an apology for an education, which his quick wit and active intelligence rapidly improved upon, he began life as clerk in a country store, where he served out sanded sugar and watered rum as prosaically as any country boy who ever aspired to the Presidency.

But his spirit was restless and he did not long remain behind the counter. As a peddler he roamed around the country vending articles of jewelry, lottery tickets and similar articles, the whole and sole end of his endeavors being, as he expressed it, to "take care of number one." At last he became a devotee of the Methodist persuasion; exhorted the sinners, led in the class meetings and shouted, sung and hallooed with the most orthodox. From Methodism to Mormonism the conversion was an easy one for him. He saw a great future in the new faith and in 1832 embraced it.

He was made an elder of the church and began to preach at the settlement at Kirtland. In 1835, as we have described, he was made an apostle and sent to do missionary work in New England. The death of Joe Smith called him from the East and he found the settlers at Nauvoo in the greatest agitation and confusion, without a leader and in doubt as to where to get one.

Not that there were no aspirants to the place, for Joe Smith had left a son who bore his name and of whom Joe Smith's wife, Emma, swore his father had had a revelation that he should be his successor. Sidney Rigdon, too, had stepped in and actually assumed the Presidency. But a stronger than either he or the dead prophet's son was destined for the place.

Young contrived to get the right side of his eleven brother apostles, however, and they elected him. Events proved the wisdom of their choice.

Joe Smith died in 1844. In 1845 the Legislature of Illinois revoked the charter of Nauvoo and the Mormons were ordered to move out. The hostile Gentiles then laid siege to the place and after a connonnade of three days Brigham and his followers struck their colors. All they asked was time enough to get somewhere where they could molest no one and where no one would molest them.

The Rocky Mountains were in those days almost the western boundary of the continent and beyond them the persecuted Mormons resolved to seek a home. Explorers were sent out at once to look for a suitable spot to locate, and brought back favorable reports of the valley of the Great Salt Lake, which had first been explored by Gen. Fremont in 1843.

To Salt Lake, then, Brigham resolved to travel.

In February, 1855, the first emigrants crossed the ice-bound Mississippi and settled for a year in Iowa, preparing for the journey. In April, 1857, Brigham set out with a pioneer party of 143 men for the new Zion.

In the fall of that year they reached Salt Lake Valley, and Brigham, from a peak of the Wasach Mountains, saw the country, and had a vision in which he was told that this was to be their future Zion, where the Temple of the Lord was again to be erected never to be removed, and that the light of the gospel was to radiate thence to all the world. That fall the city was laid out, and they immediately commenced preparing for the reception of the hosts of Zion who were to follow.

Brigham Young returned to Iowa, and in 1848 he was confirmed by a General Conference of the Church in the position to which he had been called by the people on the occasion referred to. In the same year Young returned to Salt Lake City, taking with him the great mass of the Mormons.

These people had then collected on the banks of the Missouri, opposite Council Bluffs, preparatory to their migration to the land which Brigham told them was to flow with milk and honey, equalled only by the Promised Land, which Moses was allowed to look upon but not possess.

They endured great hardships on the journey, and intense suffering after their arrival. They were short of provisions, and before they could cultivate the land they lived on beetles and grasshoppers and such nutritious wild herbs as could be found. They were very poorly clad and without shelter, and a long and dreary winter, colder than they ever before experienced, was upon them. Was it surprising that they murmured?

But out of all their difficulties Brigham Young managed to deliver them. As soon as it could be done the people commenced agricultural pursuits. But when the husbandmen could not work they were employed in other ways, and such as could not labor advantageously on any necessary work, were made to labor on the "Bulwarks of Zion."

Utah being in the very centre of the Indian country, the Mormons were from the first subject to savage assaults. Consequently wherever

WORKING HARD TO SAVE (?) A SOUL.

SAVED!

a settlement was made, the first work was to build a fort. Danger did not daunt the saints, however. They could fight as well as toil.

Nothing better proves the ability of Brigham Young as the leader of a fanatical religious sect, and as a man of most extraordinary resources, than the management of the migration of the Mormons and of their affairs during the first year of their arrival in the valley.

At that time Utah was a part of Mexico. By a treaty between that Government and the United States the territory was ceded to the latter, and in 1849 the Mormons met in convention, adopted a constitution which they called "The Constitution of the State of Deseret," and applied for immediate admission into the Union under it. There was then no recognized government in that country; but the year following Congress organized the present territory, and Mr. Fillmore, who was then President, appointed Brigham Young the first Governor as well as Commissioner of Indian Affairs.

From the organization of the territory in 1850 in 1857, nothing remarkable in the history of the saints occurred. Then came those events which led to the invasion of the territory by General (then Colonel) Sidney Johnson.

These events can be briefly told. The Government, when it made Brigham Governor, appointed also District Judges, who established United States Courts in the Territory. The Mormons viewed them with much suspicion, and finally drove them out of the State in 1851. The Government then suspended Brigham Young from his office as Governor and sent Colonel Steptole, U. S. A., out to succeed him. He arrived in Utah in 1854, but found it safe to withdraw from a country he saw no chance of governing. For two years more the Mormons and the United States officers wrangled, till, in 1856, the latter were forced to flee from the Territory.

The Government now appointed Alfred Cuming Governor, and sent him out with 2,000 regular soldiers, under Colonel Albert Sidney Johnston, to seat him in power.

Brigham Young refused to furnish supplies for the troops and issued his proclamation declaring martial law, and calling out the militia.

The army advanced to near where Fort Bridger now stands, when their supplies became scant for the winter. While there Brigham addressed a communication to Colonel Johnston, warning him to leave the territory, but in the event Colonel Johnston desired to remain over winter, he might "do so in peace and unmolested," provided he would deposit his arms and ammunition with the Quartermaster-General of the territory, and, "leave in the spring, or as soon as the roads would permit him to march."

It is unnecessary to add that neither modest **request was** complied with.

While the **army was** approaching, the **Mormons** were fortifying Echo Canon, to prevent its penetrating further into the territory. The only act of hostility committed **during the** campaign **was the** destruction of two supply trains, belonging to Johnston's army. This was done by a **band of** horsemen, **supposed to have** been commanded by Porter Rockwell, who **figures conspicuously in** Mormon history **as one** of the Danites, or "avenging angels," **and of whom I shall** write later.

General Johnston was not acting under orders to **attack** the Mormons, **and** this act of **hostility** would have been a most excellent pretext for accepting war, and **then** and forever settling the question of Mormonism in our country, was not taken advantage of. **Neither the** defences of Echo Canon, **nor** the size of the Mormon army, were by any means the cause **of it not being.** But the **army was short of** supplies, as I have already said, and **a campaign in such a** country under the circumstances was out of **the question.**

Johnston remained through the **winter, negotiating, with the result** that the Mormons admitted **Governor Cuming** to his seat. **The troops** remained in camp till **1860, when they returned to** the **states.** The civil war diverted attention from **the** saints and they had pretty much their **own** way **till** the end. **Then the** government began to pay some attention to them again, **and in 1871** went so far as **to** declare polygamy a crime **and arrest** Brigham. **He was** released and died on August 29th, **1877, in** his latter years having **been much** curtailed by his powers.

Brigham **left 17** wives and 56 children, and a fortune of $2,000,000 to support them. **In** 1874 one of his wives, Ann Eliza Young, the 15th, had received a divorce from him in the United States courts.

Such, in brief, is the history of the greatest man Mormonism has ever produced. Now for a glance at some of the crimes he fathered.

CHAPTER VIII.

THE CRIMES OF MORMONISM.

No history of a savage African king, throned on the bodies of his slaughtered victims, is blackened by more shameful crimes than the chronicles of Mormonism, and no crime in Mormon records is more atrocious than that whose auther was, in 1877, shot to death upon the scene of the massacre he directed. I allude to the crime and the expiation of Bishop John D. Lee.

In the summer of 1857, a large train, with emigrants for California, consisting of men, women and children to the number of about one hundred and forty persons, passed through Salt Lake City, and proceeded southward on the usual route to Los Angelos, when they reached Mountain Meadows, a valley in a sparsely settled country, about three hundred miles south of Salt Lake City.

Their stock was first run off by what appeared to be Indians, but really by Mormons disguised as such, and under command of Lee, who was acting by Brigham Young's orders. Their enemies making hostile demonstrations, the emigrants got together their wagons, and throwing up earth about them made a work of defence.

Their assailants occupied the hills around, and fought them for several days without gaining any advantage. Finding it impossible to capture them without serious loss, they resorted to strategy and deception.

Several prominent Mormons took a wagon and went around so as to approach the emigrants from the head of the meadows and as they did so exhibited a red flag. The emigrants recognizing white men in the wagon allowed them to approach and held up a little girl dressed in white to answer the signal. The Mormons entered the fort. They represented that they had talked with the "Indians" and found them very furious—determined to capture the party at all hazards, but that they, the Mormons, would negotiate with the "Indians" for terms of surrender if it was desired.

They were requested to do so and after a short absence returned with the "Indians'" alternative—the surrender of everything and their lives would be spared. In addition to the purported agreement on the part of the assailants, as their part of the treaty, not to injure the emigrants personally, the Mormon negotiators proposed to furnish an escort of forty armed men to conduct them back to the settlements.

Harsh as were the terms they were accepted, the presence of helpless women and children influencing the emigrants in their decision. The escort arrived and the unsuspecting emigrants abandoned everything and marched out of their fort. The women and children were in front, the men behind them, and the guard in the rear of all.

In this order they marched a short distance, when at a given signal the "Indians" rushed upon the party, shooting dead by the first volley the men and afterward the women and children, except seventeen of the latter who were supposed to be too young to tell the tale of this horrid butchery. No injury was sustained by the escort.

Brigham Young, who was at the time Superintendent of Indian affairs in the territory, made no allusion to the massacre in his annual report. Nor did he for a long time refer to it in the pulpit and when he did so it was of course to deny the guilt of the Mormons.

Some years after the horrible murder Gen. Carlton marched a column of troops by the locality, when he found the bones of the slain still bleaching upon the meadow. Here and there lay a skull with the long hair attached, indicating the sex of the murdered, and interspersed with the others were the small bones of the children. Even then an officer declares the sight to have been horrible and sickening. The General had these bones collected and buried and over the spot he made a mound from which was raised a wooden cross and on it he placed the inscription: "Vengeance is mine, and I will repay, saith the Lord."

Not long after Brigham Young visited the locality and about the same time the rude monument was demolished.

But its memory lived and the inscription Brigham caused to be wiped out was prophetic. Twenty years after his crime had been accomplished and after the man who had instigated it had gone to his account, John D. Lee, in September, 1877, after a fair trial by a United States court was led out and fusiladed on the very spot the blood of his hapless victims had enriched.

Another shocking act of barbarity was the slaughter of the Morrisites. It occurred in 1862. The Morrissites were named after their leader. They were Mormons who objected to Brigham Young

A MORMON BABY FARM.

MORMON HOUSEHOLD DISCIPLINE.

THE MYSTERIES OF MORMONISM.

and who set up an independent settlement on the Weber river. A dispute arose between the Morrisites and Brighamites as to the authority of the latter to impose fines and levy taxes upon a people who claimed the same right to exercise an independent government as had those who oppressed them.

For some offence the Morrisites resisted a civil officer of Brigham's government, when the official obtained a large armed posse and again visited the settlement to serve the writ. Foolishly the Morrisites still resisted and retaining the fanaticism they had acquired under Brigham they were presumptuous enough to accept battle. Being very much in the minority they were compelled to surrender and did so, giving up their arms. The Mormon sheriff then rode into their fort, inquired for Morris, when a poor old helpless fanatic was pointed out to him, and drawing his pistol he shot him dead in cold blood. Two or three of the party were murdered in the same way.

Late in the fall of 1859 a company of California emigrants numbering eight wagons, ten men, twelve women and a little multitude of children, halted at Salt Lake City to rest and refresh themselves and their animals preparatory to crossing the Sierra Nevada. The men were shrewd and observant, the women inquisitive and they managed to ferret out some of the secrets the Mormons did not care to have carried away. It was decided to put them out of the way, and several of the saints were selected to accomplish that end.

These scoundrels hired themselves to the emigrants as guides through the Sierra Nevada.

The Sierra Nevada is not a single mountain range, but a succession of ranges and ridges, and ridges alternating with narrow glens, generally filled with torrent-like rivers and unfathomable lakes. Bewildered among these mountains escape is quite impossible. As well might one attempt to find his way to the open air through the intricate chambers of the Cretan labyrinth. One mountain crossed amid all the horrors of snow and cold and fatigue only brings you to the foot of another. Unfathomable gulfs, frozen lakes, unmeasured precipices are before and around you and the most horrid of deaths is the only relief.

Into this wilderness the Mormon guides led their victims, leaving them after having directed them *not to the West but to the North !*

The snows clos d around them and it was finally proposed to encamp and remain through the winter. They discovered a cave opening on the sheltered side of the mountain, whose icy pinnacle glittered above them at the height of 15,000 feet. Drawing their wagons up to the entrance their goods were unloaded and most of them removed to the cavern, while the cattle were turned loose to browse on the tender twigs of the stunted bushes and pick the scanty tufts of grass where the wind had blown the snow from the mountain tops. A party of five men went forward to explore the route, but after wandering hither and thither for nearly a week and subsisting on the bark of trees, they returned to the encampment no better off than when they left it. Again and again the same project was undertaken, but never with success.

One by one the cattle were killed and eaten and occasionally the hunters would bring in some game. These resources failing, roots, the bark of trees and even grass afforded the means of a scanty subsistence. But the cold became insupportable; the ground was covered with tremendous snow drifts, snow and sleet filled the air and obscured the heavens.

Some took to their beds and refused to leave them; others, whose enfeebled and emaciated limbs refused to support their weight, crawled on their hands and knees through the cold and snow to such places as the wind had left bare and dug with their stiffened and benumbed fingers for the roots of grass or anything else that could preserve life. Husbands were reduced to the necessity of feeding upon the flesh of their dead wives, and mothers, with ravenous appetite, feasted on the mangled bodies of their children.

When spring came the snows melted form a charnel house upon the mountain side. Only skeletons remained to endorse the story told in triumph in the Mormon temple of how the enemies of the church had been betrayed to death.

CHAPTER IX.

THE DANITES.

When the citizens of Carroll and Davis Counties, Mo., began to threaten the Mormons with expulsion in 1838, a "death society" was organized, under the direction of Sidney Rigdon, and with the sanction of Smith. Its first captain was Captain "Fearnot," alias David Patten, an Apostle. Its object was the punishment of the obnoxious. Some time elapsed before finding a suitable name. They desired one that should seem to combine spiritual authority, with a suitable sound. Micah, iv. 13, furnished the first name, "Arise, and thresh, O! daughter of Zion; for I will make thy horn iron, and thy hoofs brass; and thou shalt beat in pieces many people; and I will consecrate their gain unto the Lord, and their substance unto the Lord of the whole earth." This accurately described their intentions, and they called themselves the "Daughters of Zion." Some ridicule was made at these bearded and bloody "daughters," and the name did not sit easily. "Destroying Angels" came next; the "Big Fan" of the thresher that "should thoroughly purge the floor," was tried and dropped. Genesis, xlix. 17, furnished the name that they finally assumed. The verse is quite significant: "Dan shall be a serpent by the way, an adder in the path, that biteth the horse's heels, so that his rider shall fall backward." The "Sons of Dan" was the style they adopted; and many have been the times that they have been *adders in the path, and many a man has fallen backward, and has been seen no more.* At Salt Lake, among themselves, they ferociously exult in these things, rather than seek to deny or extenuate them.

When a man is missing at Salt Lake, it is a common expression, "He has met the Indians." Whenever this term was used it was understood to mean that the Danites had been at work.

It would require a volume even to furnish a catalogue of the crimes of these mysterious and deadly bravoes. The following are a few examples of their work.

Colonel Peltro and Mr. Tobin, with their servants, were severely wounded by Mormons, who attacked them in the night, on Santa Clara river, 370 miles south of Salt Lake. They lost six horses, and were compelled to abandon their baggage, which was perfectly riddled with shot. The object of their enmity and this attempted assassination was Mr. Tobin. He went with Captain Stansbury to Salt Lake in 1851; then met Brigham, and admired his daughter Alice; was engaged to her, and left Salt Lake on business. He returned in 1856, and renewed his engagement with Miss Alice; although she was at the same time under a *written* engagement to a Mr. W. Wright, whom Brigham sent off to the Sandwich Islands, to get him out of the way. Mr. Tobin told me in California that he had the most convincing proof that Miss Young had sacrificed her honor, and accordingly refused to marry her. For this Mormon hated; for the influence he might exert abroad, Mormon feared; and because both hated and feared, he was nearly Mormon murdered.

One evening in November, 1866, Dr. Robinson, a Gentile, who had lived in Salt Lake City for several years, and practiced his profession as a physician, was called by two men who represented that a friend had a fractured thigh. The doctor immediately dressed, and started on what he supposed a mission of mercy, and after proceeding a few squares was shot through the head, and died shortly afterward, remaining unconscious from the time he received the wound. Mrs. Robinson knew of the two men calling, but did not know who they were. Notwithstanding the most searching investigation on the part of the Chief Justice and the Governor, no clue whatever could be had to the murderers.

Dr. Robinson had been for some time conducting a suit against the Mormon authorities for the possession of the land upon which the Warm Springs were located, to which he claimed pre-emption right. Brigham Young also claimed the land, and as usual, Young got it.

About the time of the Robinson murder, several other citizens of Salt Lake narrowly escaped the severe vengeance of the Mormons, for an offence which is the only one Dr. Robinson is known to have committed against them—that of claiming public lands in the vicinity of Zion. These lands had not been surveyed, nor brought into market, and the parties that settled upon them considered that they were subject to the same laws that govern other unsurveyed public land. Several small tracts of these were pre-empted and occupied. Among other settlers was Dr. Williamson, who had erected a temporary building on a quarter section near the Jordan. A raid was made on all such about the same time, and their buildings destroyed. The doctor was caught, tied, and wrapped in an old tent, preparatory to making a literal Jordan his entrance way into eternity; but he was not the least disconcerted by their conduct, and very coolly informed the mob that he would prefer that they should "shoot him as they would a dog, rather than drown him as they would a cat." Whether they admired his coolness, so as to induce them to desist, or the whole was intended as a scare, I am unable to say, but they let him go.

"YOU PAYS YOUR MONEY AND TAKES YOUR CHOICE."

"THOU SHALT INCREASE AND MULTIPLY."

A young man, who had visited Utah in company with an emigrant train, became enamored of a young girl belonging to a Mormon family, though not a daughter of the house. His affections were returned with ardor by the lady, whose hand had been demanded by a Mormon elder, already the husband of nine wives. Ignorant of danger and intent only on the gratification of his passion, the lover remained in Utah while his friends prosecuted their journey. The girl, from the commencement of his attentions, had been strictly watched, yet love laughs at locksmiths, and they had concerted a plan of escape. This by some unaccountable means was betrayed, and the eloping lady leaped from the window of the room in which she was confined, not into the arms of the youth, but those of the man she loathed and hated.

But where went the lover?

These are but a few examples. It is beyond the limit of our volume to give more than a suggestion of the monstrous outrages on humanity which the bravoes of the Mormon Church were guilty of. History has recorded many of them, and when the crash comes and the Mormon monstrosity is swept from the earth, there will be men enough found to reveal the secrets of a power they no longer fear.

One other fact I must dwell upon in connection with the Danites though. That is the frequency with which they were employed against a sex whose weakness should have been their best safeguard.

Let a woman, if she dare, commit such acts as would be likely to bring polygamy into disrepute, expose the weakness or sensuality of an elder, or manifest a disapprobation to the existing state of things, and some hideous punishment would be sure to be hers—when, where, or what, it would be impossible to tell, though none the less hideous and certain—that is, if information of it ever reached the ears of the elect and sanctified.

One poor woman who had told an emigrant in the hearing of a Mormon elder that polygamy was a system of abominations, and who repeated a few of her troubles and sufferings, was taken one night when she stepped out for water, gagged, carried a mile into the woods, stripped nude, tied to a tree, and scourged till the blood ran from her wounds to the ground, in which condition she was left till the next night, when her tormentors visited her again, took her back to her husband's residence and laid her on the doorstep, where she remained till morning. She remained sick for a long time. Her husband's other wives refused to nurse and care for her, and she finally died, after lingering something more than a year.

Another female was suddenly snatched up by a man on horseback, when returning to her home in the dusk of the evening, carried to a retired place, and her mouth and tongue seared with a red-hot iron, though they refused to inform her in what she had offended, and she could remember nothing. Having thus mutilated her they carried her fifty miles out into the prairie and left her to wander, naked, till she starved. She was found, nearly dead, by a party of emigrants, and her barbarous torture made known to the world in writing, as she had lost the power of speech.

Such things, I may add, were not solitary acts, but of frequent occurrence, and the female part of the population were in a state of constant apprehension.

It must be understood that, though I write in the past tense of the Danites, their organization exists to-day as strong as ever, and as ready to perform the functions of its dark office. Porter Rockwell is dead, but he has left successors.

Who is Porter Rockwell? Porter Rockwell was the most dreaded leader of the Danites, or "Avenging Angels." How many he caused to disappear mysteriously, or be killed by the Indians when the Indians were committing no depredations, cannot be told, but Porter Rockwell enjoyed his infamous life for many years in savage impunity.

In his latter days he became a drunkard, and used to wander the streets of Salt Lake City looking for fight. He seldom got it though. Scores of men who would willingly have shot him down held their hands in fear of the vengeance this act of justice might invoke on them.

Blood atonement, all denials to the contrary, is practiced to-day as frequently as it was twenty-five years ago, though not so openly. There are no Coroners in Utah, and when a body is in death it is simply buried. Poison does the work, and there are no inquiries. When a man gets tired of his wife he poisons her, if he anticipates the least trouble in obtaining a divorce.

Mrs. Maxwell came to Salt Lake City with her husband in 1869. Two years afterward her husband took another wife, and one year subsequently he was sealed to a third. Mrs. Maxwell had two sons, aged respectively fourteen and sixteen years. Their father urged them to go through the Endowment House and become Mormons, bound by all the oaths of the church. Mrs. Maxwell objected, and in order to prevail over her sons she told them the secrets of the Endowment House.

The penalty for revealing these secrets is dismemberment of the body, the throat cut, and tongue torn out.

Mr. Maxwell overheard his wife, being in an adjoining room, and forthwith he informed the Elders, who sent for the unfortunate woman and her two sons. They were taken into what is called the "dark pit," a blood atoning room under Brigham Young's house. The woman was then stripped of all her clothing, and then tied on her back to a large table. Six members of the priesthood then performed their damnable crime; they first cut off their victim's tongue, they then cut her throat, after which her legs and arms were severed.

The sons were compelled to stand by and witness this dreadful slaughter of their mother. They were then released and given twenty-four hours to get out of the territory, which was then an impossibility. The sons went directly to the house of a friend, to whom they related the butchery of their mother, and obtaining a package of provisions they started; but on the following morning they were both dead.

They had met the Danites.

Created in the most sombre secrecy, this infamous organization was from the first a shadowy terror known only by its works. The real calling of a "Destroying Angel" is rarely known save among his fellows. To the bulk of the people to whom he is a constant menace, the assassin of the church is a mere spectre, red handed, merciless and deadly, but invisible and therefore the more dreadful. Your murderer might be your own brother, and you never dream it, so well are the secrets of this shameful order kept.

An instance of this: One day in Salt Lake City I was out walking with a male relative, and a man stopped us. During the conversation I observed him closely, because he was so handsome—with light, wavy brown hair, skin like a girl's, and beautiful blue eyes. He was tall and of slender build. He was dressed after the fashion of men in general, except that he wore a large sombrero, which he kept drawn well over his face. He conversed affably, his voice being noticeably melodious. After he went his way my cousin said:

"Well, you have seen one at last."

"One what?" I asked.

"An Avenging Angel."

"Where, where?" I said, looking around.

"Why, the man who has just left us. He is the chief Avenging Angel, and has had a hand in the bloodiest deeds that have stained the record of this Territory."

In after years I was fated to have experience enough with these men of blood, and the very one I met that day was destined to become a persecutor from whose ruthless hand chance alone saved me.

CHAPTER X.

SECRETS OF THE ENDOWMENT HOUSE.

The Mormon Endowment House of Salt Lake is a plain adobe building, two stories high, built like a small dwelling-house, so as not to attract attention. There are blinds to all the windows, which are nearly always kept down. It is situated in the northwest corner of the Temple block (which includes the Tabernacle, New Temple, etc.), and the whole block is surrounded by a very high wall.

On a certain day, not necessary to mention, I went to the Endowment House at eight o'clock in the morning, taking with me my endowment clothes (consisting of garments, robe, cap, apron and moccasins). I went into a small room attached to the main building (designated by the name of reception room), which was crowded with men and women having their bundles of clothing. The entrance door is on the east side, and in the southwest corner; there is another, next to which the desk stood, where the clerk recorded the names, etc. Around the north and west sides were benches for the people to sit.

On going up to the desk, I presented my recommendation from the bishop in whose ward I was staying, and George Reynolds, who was acting as clerk, asked me my name, those of my parents, when and where I was born, and when I was baptized in the Mormon Church.

That over, he told me to leave my hat, cloak and shoes in that room; and taking up my bundle, I went into another room, where I sat waiting till it came my turn to be washed.

WAITING FOR THE OLD MAN.

A MORMON; HOME RULER.

One of the women, an officiating high priestess, told me to come behind the curtain, where I could hear a great deal of splashing and subdued conversation. I went, and after I was undressed, I had to step into a long bath, about half full of water, when another woman proceeded to wash me. I objected strongly to this part of the business, but was told to show a more humble spirit. However, when she got down to my feet, she let me go, and I was turned over to the woman who had spoken to me first, and whose name was Bethsheba Smith (one of the widows of Apostle George A. Smith). She wore a large shiny apron, and her sleeves tucked up above her elbows. She looked thoroughly like business.

Another woman was standing beside her with a large wooden spoon and some green olive oil in a cow's horn. This woman poured the oil out of the spoon into Bethsheba's hand, who immediately put it on my head, ears, eyes, mouth and every part of my body, and as she greased me, she muttered a kind of prayer over each member of my body: My head that I might have a knowledge of the truths of God; my eyes, that I might see the glories of the kingdom; my mouth, that I might at all times speak the truth; my arms, that they might be strong in the defense of the gospel, etc. She finally got down to my feet, which she hoped might be swift in the paths of righteousness and truth.

She then turned me over to the woman who had washed me, and who whispered my new and celestial name in my ear. I believe I am to be called up in the morning of the resurrection by it. It was "Sarah." I felt disappointed. I thought I should have received a more distinguished name. She told me that the new name must never be spoken, but often thought of, to keep away evil spirits. I should be required to speak it once that day, but she would tell me in what part of the ceremony, and that I should never again have to speak it.

She then told me to put on my garments. These are made in one piece. On the right breast is a square, on the left a compass, in the centre a small hole, and on the knee a large hole, which is called the "Stone." We were told that as long as we kept them on no harm could befall us, and that when we changed them we were not to take them all off at once, but slip out a limb at a time and immediately dive into the clean ones. The neck was never to be cut low, or the sleeves short, as that would be patterning after the fashions of the Gentiles.

After this I put on my clothes and in my stocking feet waited with those who were washed and anointed until she had finished the remaining two or three. This done, the little calico curtains were drawn aside and the men and women stood revealed to each other. The men looked very uncomfortable, and not at all picturesque. They only had their garments and shirts on, and they really did seem as though they were ashamed of themselves, as well they might be.

Joseph F. Smith then came to where we were all waiting, and told us that if "we wanted to back out, now was our time," because we should not be able afterward, and that we were bound to go right through. All those who wanted to go through were to hold up their hands, which of course everyone did, believing that all the good and holy things that were to be seen and heard were yet to come. He then told us that if ever any of us attempted to reveal what we saw and heard in the "House," our memories would be blighted, for they were things too holy to be spoken of between each other, after we had once left the Endowment House. We were then told to be very quiet and listen. Joseph F. Smith then went away.

In a few moments we heard voices talking loudly, so that the people could hear them in the adjoining room. (I afterward found out in passing through that it was the prayer circle room). It was supposed to be conversation between Elohim and Jehovah. The conversation was as follows:

Elohim to Jehovah: "Well, Jehovah, I think we will create an earth; let Michael go down and collect all the elements together and found one."

Answer: "Very well; it shall be done."

Then, calling to another man, we could hear him say:

"Michael, go down and collect all the elements together and form an earth, and then report to us what you have done."

Answer: "Very well."

The man they called Michael then left the prayer circle room and came through the room they called the World, into the Garden of Eden, the door of which was shut that faced the places where we were standing, listening and waiting. He remained there a second or two, and everything was quiet. At the end of that time we heard him going back the same way to where Elohim and Jehovah were waiting. When he got back he said, "I have collected all the elements together and

THE MYSTERIES OF MORMONISM.   45

founded an earth; what wouldst thou have me do next?" Using the same formula every time they sent him down to the World, they then told him to separate the land from water, light from darkness, etc., and so they went regularly through the creation, but they always told him to come up and report what he had done.

When the creation was supposed to be finished, Michael went back and told them it was very fair and beautiful to look upon. Elohim then said to Jehovah that he thought they had better go down and have a look at it, which they did and agreed with Michael that it was a beautiful place; that it seemed a pity it should be of no particular use, but thought it would be a good idea to create man to live in it and cultivate these things.

They then came out of the Garden of Eden (which was supposed to have been newly finished), and shutting the door after them came to where we were standing. We were then told to shut our eyes, and Jehovah said to Michael, "Give me a handful of dust and I will create man." We were then told to open our eyes, and we saw a man that he had taken from the crowd, standing beside Jehovah, and to whom Jehovah said: "I will call thee Adam, for thou shalt be the father of all mankind." Jehovah then said it was not good for man to be alone, so he would create a woman and a helpmate for him. We were again told to close our eyes, and Adam was requested to go to sleep, which he obligingly did. Jehovah was then supposed to take a rib from Adam's side and form Eve. We were then told to open our eyes and look upon the handiwork of the Lord. When we did we saw a woman taken from the crowd who was standing by Adam's side. Jehovah said he would call the woman Eve, because she would be the mother of all mankind.

The door of the Garden of Eden was then opened, and we all marched in with our little bundles (the men going first, as they always take precedence), and we all ranged ourselves round the room on benches. The four sides of this room are painted in imitation of trees, flowers, birds, wild beasts, etc. (The artist who painted the room was evidently more acquainted with whitewashing than painting). The ceiling was painted blue, dotted over with golden stars; in the centre of it was the sun, a little further along, the moon, and all around were the stars. In each corner was a Masonic emblem. In one corner is a compass, in another the square, the remaining two were the level and the plumb. On the east side of the room, next the door, was a printed apple tree, and in the northeast part of the room was a small wooden altar.

After we had seated ourselves, Jehovah told Adam and Eve that they could eat of every tree in the garden except of this particular apple tree, for on the day that they ate of that they should surely die.

He then took his departure, and immediately after in came a very lively gentleman, dressed in a plain black morning suit, with a little apron on, a most fiendish expression on his face, and joyfully rubbing his hands. This gentleman was supposed to be "the demon." Certainly his appearance made the supposition quite easy; by-the-bye, I have since seen that same gentleman administering the Sacrament in the Tabernacle on Sundays. He went up to Eve and remarked that it was a very beautiful place, and that the fruit was so nice, would she like to taste one of those apples? She demurred a little, and said she was told not to, and therefore musn't. But he pretended to pluck one of the painted apples and give it to her, and she pretended to eat it. He then told her to ask Adam to have some, and she did. Adam objected strongly to tasting, knowing the penalty, but Eve eventually overcame his scruples, saying: "Oh, my dear, they're so nice, you haven't any idea; and that nice old gentleman here (pointing to the demon) says that he can recommend them and you need not be afraid of what Jehovah says."

Adam consented, and immediately after he said, "Oh, what have I done, and how foolish I was to listen to you!" He then said that he could see himself, and that they had no clothes on, and they must sew some fig-leaves together. Every one then made a dive for his apron out of the little bundles. This apron is a square half yard of green silk with nine fig-leaves worked on it in brown sewing silk. A voice was then heard calling for Adam, who pretended to hide, when in came Jehovah. He gave Adam a good scolding, but finally told him that he would give him certain instructions, whereby he would have a chance to regain the presence of his Father after he was driven out into the world. These instructions consisted of grips, etc., and the garments he wore would protect him from all evil. (Mormons say of these garments that the pattern was revealed direct from heaven to Joseph Smith, and are the same as were originally worn by Adam).

They then put on their caps and moccasins, the women's caps

VERILY, HE WAS IN LUCK.

A CANDIDATE FOR ADMISSION.

THE MYSTERIES OF MORMONISM.   47

being made of Swiss muslin, one yard square, rounded at one corner so as to fit the head, and with strings on it which tie under the chin. The moccasins are made of linen or calico. The men's are made exactly like those of pastry cooks, with a bow on the right side. I should here mention before I go further, that Bethsheba Smith and one of the priests enacted the parts of Adam and Eve, and so stood sponsors for the rest of us, who were individually supposed to be Adams and Eves.

They then proceeded to give us the first grip of the Aaronic or Lesser Priesthood, which consists on putting the thumb on the knuckle of the index finger, and clasping the hands round. We were then made to swear "To obey the laws of the Mormon Church and all they enjoin, in preference to those of the United States." The penalty for revealing this grip and oath is, that you will have your throat cut from ear to ear, and your tongue torn from your mouth, and the sign of the penalty is drawing the hand with the thumb pointing toward the throat sharply across, and bringing the arm to the level of the square, and, with the hand upraised to heaven, swearing to abide the same.

We were then driven out of this into the room called the world, where there were three men standing at a small altar on the east side of the room, who were supposed to represent Peter, James and John, Peter standing in the centre. He was supposed to have the keys of heaven. Men representing (or trying to) the different religious sects, then came and presented their views, and said they wanted to try and save those fallen children. In doing this they could not refrain from exaggerating and coarsely satirizing the different sects they represented.

Then the demon came in and tried to allure the people, and bustling up to the altar, Peter said to him: "Hello, Mr. Demon, how do you do to-day! It's a very fine day, isn't it? What have you come after?" The demon replied that he didn't seem to take to any of these so-called Christian religions, why didn't they quit bothering after anything of the kind, and live a life of pleasure, etc.? However, he was told to go, and that quickly.

Peter then gave the second grip of the Aaronic or Lesser Priesthood, which consists of putting the thumb between the knuckles of the index and second fingers, and clasping the hand around. The penalty for revealing this is to be sawn asunder, and our members cast into the sea. The sign of the penalty was drawing the hand sharply across the middle of the body. To receive the grip we had to put on our robes, which consists of a long, straight piece of cloth reaching to our feet, doubled over and gathered very full on the shoulder and round the waist. There was also a long, narrow piece of cloth tied around the waist called "the sash." It was placed on the right shoulder to receive this grip. The people wear their aprons over it. The men then took the oath of chastity and the women the same; they don't consider polygamy at all unchaste, but said that it was a heaven-ordained law, and that a man, to be exalted in the world to come, must have more than one wife. The women then took the oath of obedience to their husbands, having to look up to them as their gods. It is not possible for a woman to go to heaven, except through her husband.

Then a man came in and said that the Gospel (which during those few minutes' intervals had lain dormant for eighteen hundred years) had been again restored to earth, and that an angel had revealed it to a young boy named Joseph Smith, and that all the gifts, blessings and prophecies of old had been restored with it, and this last revelation was to be called the Latter-day Dispensation. The priests pretended joyfully to accept this, and said it was the very thing they were in search of, nothing else having had the power to satisfy them.

They then proceeded to give us the first grip of the Melchizedek or Higher Priesthood. The thumb is placed on the knuckle of the index finger, and the index finger is placed straight along the palm of the hand, while the lower part of the hand is clasped with the remaining fingers. The robe for this grip was changed from the right to the left shoulder. We were then made to swear to avenge the death of Joseph Smith, the martyr, together with that of his brother, Hiram, on this American nation, and that we would teach our children and children's children to do so. The penalty for this grip and oath was disembowelment.

We were then marched into the northeast room (the men, of course, always going first) designated the prayer circle room. We were here made to take an oath of obedience to the Mormon priesthood.

And now the highest or grand grip of the Melchizedek priesthood was given. We clasped each other round the hand with the point of the index finger resting on the wrist, and little fingers firmly linked together.

The men then formed a circle round the altar, linking their arms straight across and placed their hands on one another's shoulders. The priest knelt at the altar and took hold of one of the men's hands and prayed. He told us that the electric current of prayer passed through that circle, and that was the most efficatious kind of prayer. The women stood outside the circle with their vails covering their faces, the only time throughout the ceremony that they did so.

The prayer over, they all trooped up the staircase on the north side of the house, into the room called the Instruction Room, where the people sat down on benches on the west side of the room. Facing them about midway between floor and ceiling was a wooden beam that went across the room from north to south, and from which was suspended a dirty-looking piece of what was once white calico. This was called "The Vail," and is supposed to be in imitation of the one in Solomon's Temple. On this vail are marks like those on the garments, together with extra holes for putting the arms through, and a hole at the top to speak through. But before going through the vail, we received a general outline of the instructions we had received down stairs. This over, the priest took a man to the vail to one of the openings, where he knocked with a small wooden mallet that hung on the wooden support. A voice on the other side the vail (it was supposed to be Peter's) asked who was there, when the priest answering for the man, said: "Adam, having been faithful, desires to enter." The priest then led the man up to the west side of the vail, where he had to put his hands through and clasp the man, or Peter (to whom he whispered his new name, and the only one he ever tells, for they must never tell their celestial names to their wives, although the wives must tell theirs to their husbands), through the holes in the vail. He was then allowed to go through to the other side, which was supposed to be heaven, and this is where a strong imagination might be of some use, for anything more unlike heaven I can't conceive. The man having got through, he went to opening No. 2, and told the gatekeeper to call for the woman he was about to marry, telling him her name. She then stepped up to the vail. They could not see each other, but put their hands through the openings, one of their hands on each other's shoulders and the other around the waist.

With hands so fixed, the knees were placed within each other, the feet, of course, being the same, the woman's given name was then whispered through the vail, then her new and celestial name, the priestess who stood by to instruct the woman told them to repeat after her a formula or oath. The last and highest grip of the Melchizedek priesthood was then given through the vail.

They then released their hold of each other, and the priestess, taking the woman to opening No. 2, knocked the same as they did at the men's entrance, and the gatekeeper having asked "Who is there," and the priestess having replied, "Eve, having been faithful in all things, desires to enter." Eve was accordingly ushered into heaven.

Before I go farther, I must tell how they believe the entrance into heaven is to be gained on the morning of the resurrection. Peter will call up the men and the women (for it is not possible for a woman to be resurrected or exalted in heaven unless some man takes pity on her and raises her). If the marks on the garment are found to correspond with those on the vail (the dead are buried in the whole paraphernalia) if you can give the grips and tokens, and your new name, and are dressed properly in your robes; why, then, one has a sure permit to heaven, and will pass by the angels (who they suppose are to be only ministering servants) to a more exalted glory; the more wives they, they think, the higher their glory will be.

To resume: After we got through, we saw Joseph F. Smith sitting at a table recording the names of those who were candidates for marriage. He wrote the names in a book (the existence of which marriage register this truthful apostle has since denied, so that a polygamous marriage could not be found out), and then he wrote the two names on a slip of paper, to be taken into the sealing room to the officiating priest, so that he might know whom he was marrying. After having given this slip of paper to the priest (Daniel H. Wells), we knelt at a little wooden altar (they are all alike in the Endowment House). He then asks the man if he is willing to take the woman to wife, and the woman if she is willing to take him for a husband. They both having answered yes, he tells the man that he must look to God, but the woman must look to her husband as her god, for if he lives his religion the spirit of God will be in him, and she must therefore yield him unquestioning obedience, for he is a god unto her, and then concludes by saying that he having authority from on high to bind and loose here upon earth, and whatsoever he binds here shall be bound in heaven, seals the man and woman for time and all eternity.

THE OLD WIFE AND THE NEW.

A "CULLUD" MORMON.

He then tells the man and woman to kiss each other across the altar, the man kneeling on the north side and the woman on the south, and so it is finished. Sometimes they have witnesses, sometimes not; if they think any trouble may arise from a marriage or that the woman is inclined to be a little perverse, they have no witnesses, neither do they give marriage certificates, and if occasion requires it, and it is to shield any of their polygamous brethren from being found out, they will positively swear that they did not perform any marriage at all, so that the women in this church have but a very poor outlook for being considered honorable wives.

When the marriage ceremony was over we came out of the "sealing room." I crossed into the ladies' dressing room, where, after having dressed and my husband paid the fees, we took our departure.

It was 3:30 p. m. when we left, I having gone there at 8 o'clock in the morning. You can probably imagine how fatigued one feels, after listening patiently all the time to their incessant talking. I should, perhaps, have remarked before that the priests, when going through the House, wear their ordinary clothing, and come straight into the "House of the Lord" with their dirty boots on, as though they had just come off a farm, while we poor sinners were obliged to walk in our stocking feet lest the floor should be defiled.

People are generally baptized a day or two before they go through the "House." I was baptized the night before. On this same evening I was told that, as I was going through the "House" on the following day, I must pay the very strictest attention to everything I should see and hear, as it would be for my benefit hereafter. I was obedient in that respect, for I remember everything that happened as vividly as though it were yesterday, and if it has not been for my benefit, I hope that this book may prove of some use in warning and enlightening people as to that most horrid blasphemy, jargon and mummery that goes on in that most sacred "House of the Lord."

CHAPTER XI.

MORMON WIVES.

The most fascinating portion of Mormonism to the general outsider is undoubtedly that in which the Mormon women are concerned. The condition of the Mormon wife has been frequently described by both sides. Let these facts from experience speak for themselves.

As a general thing women are wooed in Utah the same as elsewhere. At the same time there is a class of girls who cast about and pick up a husband for themselves. When I say a husband I mean a husband, for they prefer to see how a man treats his wife and the style in which he supports her before they marry him. They don't care to experiment with a single man. They select a man of wealth, and by means of the confessional of which I have spoken, or otherwise, it is made known to him that he must marry a certain girl. It is only just to the Mormon women at large to say that this sort of girl is in the minority. Polygamy compels her to remain respectable in spite of herself, for nowhere is a lapse from virtue more condemned than among the Mormons, and the infidelity of a wife is punished by the loss of caste and complete social banishment. A woman can only be married to one man at a time. Divorce is within easy reach, but to the husband de facto and pro tem. she must remain true. A case occurred within my knowledge which, though painful, had its amusing side.

A man had a wife. Both believed polygamy was right, but when the husband put it into practice and brought home a younger and handsomer bride, the first wife found it hard to bear. There are certain things very galling about this Mormon custom. The first wife is expected to treat the new comer as a welcome guest, and if not in good circumstances she must resign her sleeping apartment to her—there's no humiliation spared the supplanted wife. She must not only get down from her own throne, but she must place her rival upon it; all of which the wife did of whom I tell you. She set her teeth so hard that no murmur escaped them, and became what Mormon women all think the Lord intended they should be, martyrs. The second wife was a pretty, addle-pated little creature, who had only married Mr. Black for the sake of a home, without caring for him in the least, while the first wife loved him devotedly. All went quietly for a time, till Mr. Black attained the grand object of a Mormon's ambition. He was given what they call a mission; that is, he was sent abroad to proselyte. In his absence the two wives lived together, and the second wife attracted the attention of an inferior man.

The first wife was all amiability to the second wife, especially when the inferior gentleman called. She discreetly withdrew, and never seemed aware that the two had fallen madly in love with each other. So matters went on until the return of the mutual husband. Wife No. 2 found a confession obligatory. The husband could not have been more astonished if the heavens had fallen, and raved more about a wife's shame and a husband's honor than Othello himself. What was to be done? A husband's honor must not be tarnished, a wife's faithlessness must be avenged. With a grim smile wife No. 1 saw wife No. 2 driven from home disgraced; for though the outraged husband speedily divorced her, the inferior gentleman refused to make an honest woman of one who had publicly been pronounced the reverse, and, driven from pillar to post, the poor creature became an outcast, and so continued until her child became a beautiful and sturdy boy. Taking him by the hand one day, she went to wife No. 1, and implored her to take him and rear him properly, "but do not separate us," she said; "give me shelter too, and I will be your servant, your willing, uncomplaining slave until death." And so they all live together, the mother in the kitchen, the son in the parlor, hardly daring to speak to each other, the divorced wife the hard-driven menial of the woman whose equal she once was, and the husband, though tolerating her presence for humanity's sake, never permitting her to speak to him.

I was invited once to dine in Salt Lake City and was introduced to a gentleman. We will call him Jones. I was also introduced to two ladies named Jones, but it did not occur to me until I was told afterward that they were both married to him. One was *passe*, proud and stately in bearing and appearance. The other was young, very pretty, and seemed to shrink at the sound of the other's voice. She flew to obey her commands, which consisted of orders to wait on Mr. Jones. "Emma," she would say, "hand George this, hand George that; get George's hat; get George's cane; fetch George's gloves," &c.

As I have said before, the first wife is mistress of all the others, and they are forced to obey her as abjectively as slaves. Emma was the second wife of Jones, and the wife ruled her with a rod of iron. There was no tyranny she did not inflict upon her, no mean, merciless grinding under foot that she did not exercise. Jones left them to fight it out. So hideous was the first wife's treatment of the second that she finally went crazy, and had to be confined in an asylum. Mrs. Jones the first urbanely gave Mr. Jones permission to bring home any number of young and pretty wives, but at latest dates he had not availed himself of her kindness.

Fighting it out reminds me of a young fellow who had a pretty young wife, but soon began to pay his addresses to a young lady. He took the latter on a little excursion, on which, as it happened, his wife had gone. They met, and, as the wife had had no intimation of what he was contemplating, she began to make a scene, just as a Gentile wife would. He hurried both ladies into a room in a rustic hotel on the pretext of talking it over quietly. As soon as he got them there he slipped out, locked them in, and gave orders below that no one should let them out or pay any attention to their cries for assistance. The day went on, and the husband enjoyed himself, but the women fought and stormed and went into hysterics and fainted and recovered and finally got awfully hungry. In vain they shouted and begged to be released. Then they wept and made up, and when the husband came and demanded through the keyhole if they were good friends and would like something to eat, they both said "Yes" meekly to all his questions. Then he unlocked the door, and they went and had a cosey little dinner together, and when he married the young lady they were all happy ever after, that is if you can believe the husband and the priests.

These sensible marriages are not always so arbitrarily made, though. I knew two schoolmates who vowed that nothing would ever part them—neither marriage nor death. When one received an eligible offer of marriage she would only accept it on condition that her husband should marry her friend before the honeymoon was over. He promised, hoping that she would change her mind, but she did not and in three weeks' time there was a second wedding. The two friends were thus happily united for life. Truly the ways of Mormon women pass all understanding. I knew one man who married two sisters at the same time, one ceremony sufficing to make him the husband of both.

THE WIVES OF A WEALTHY MORMON.

THE WIVES OF A POOR MORMON.

Although all women work in the Territory, their work is seldom of a character to increase wealth, and, as each wife must have her separate rooms or house and a stipulated allowance to live upon, it can readily be seen that polygamy was an ingenious device to keep men from amassing wealth. I remember well a case in point. The editor of a certain paper was allowed to live in peace and happiness with his only wife until the growing influence of the journal and the emoluments therefrom attracted Brigham's attention. The editor was informed one day that he had too long neglected the religious rites of the church—that he must take another wife. The editor did not want to, and, as may be supposed, neither was his wife anxious that he should. But there was no resisting Brigham. It must be done. The wife and husband were tenderly attached. They desired to keep their means for the education and future maintenance of their only son, but their private wishes availed nothing. A young girl was selected as the second wife, and a wing was built to their house. The wife fell sick with grieving and with jealous torture. As she lay for weeks on her bed she could hear the hammering going on, and listened with the same feelings that a condemned man hears the erection of the scaffold on which he is to be executed. But being a true Mormon, and believing like her husband that he was only performing a religious duty, she prayed for resignation and submission. She succeeded so well that she was able to attend the wedding, and give the bride away, as it were, but after that matters did not work well. Although the first wife tried hard to keep the peace, the second wife was a virago, and jealous of the love that the husband had evidently not transferred.

For some time the two wives lived, one in one wing of the house, the other in the other. They would meet in the back yard, common to both, several times daily, but without speaking. After the birth of a son to the second wife, her temper, because she could not entirely supplant the first wife, became so unbearable that the unlucky editor implored Young to grant him a divorce. After that the second wife went to what is popularly known as the bad. The husband induced her to give the child into the keeping of the first wife. The two boys have been reared as brothers, and no other wife has since disturbed the harmony of the little household.

Divorce is granted for infidelity and ill-treatment. In church divorces the defendant is generally reprimanded for the first offence.

A Mormon is not granted a divorce except for good cause, and being simply tired of a woman is not considered sufficient, but no Mormon of influence is unable to obtain a divorce, cause or not, if he wants it.

As the Mormons are a most prolific people, every divorced woman having two or three children by a different husband, and the husband having so many children by different wives, their relations sometimes get so mixed that no one could understand them. One man I was acquainted with married a divorced woman with three little girls, all under the age of seven. When the girls grew up he married all three, thus becoming the husband of four women, though he had but one mother-in-law, that mother-in-law being his own wife. But this is easy compared to some of their problems of relationship, which they almost go crazy themselves trying to work out. Here, for example: A man married a woman with a daughter nearly grown. When she reached womanhood, she was married to the father of her mother's husband, making him his step-daughter's step-son, and when a son was born to the father, the mother's husband became half brother to his own grandchild. The original pair also had a child—but this is getting so mixed, like everything else in Utah, that I leave it to wiser heads than mine to work out.

Of the men who first went to the Territory it is estimated that they averaged forty children each. Orson Pratt, when I last saw him, was about 80 years of age. He had more wives than any of them. On a little farm about fifteen miles from Salt Lake City, I saw his last wife. She was a fine woman, about 28 years of age, with three or four little towheaded children running about. She was terribly ignorant, while he was the most learned man in the Territory. Coming into the city the same day, I met three beautifully dressed, and, I was informed, finely educated elderly ladies. They were pointed out to me as Orson Pratt's wives. A day or two after I got into a street car. It was so loaded down entirely by ladies that I had to stand. They were all Orson Pratt's wives. A few of them went on an excursion one day, leaving the children behind. There were four wagon loads of Orson Pratt's wives, and I began to think they were as countless as the sands of the seashore.

While old men invariably select young women as wives, they often make a concession to a daughter and marry her mother at the same time, so as not to separate them, and a young man will often take

THE MORMON REBECCA.

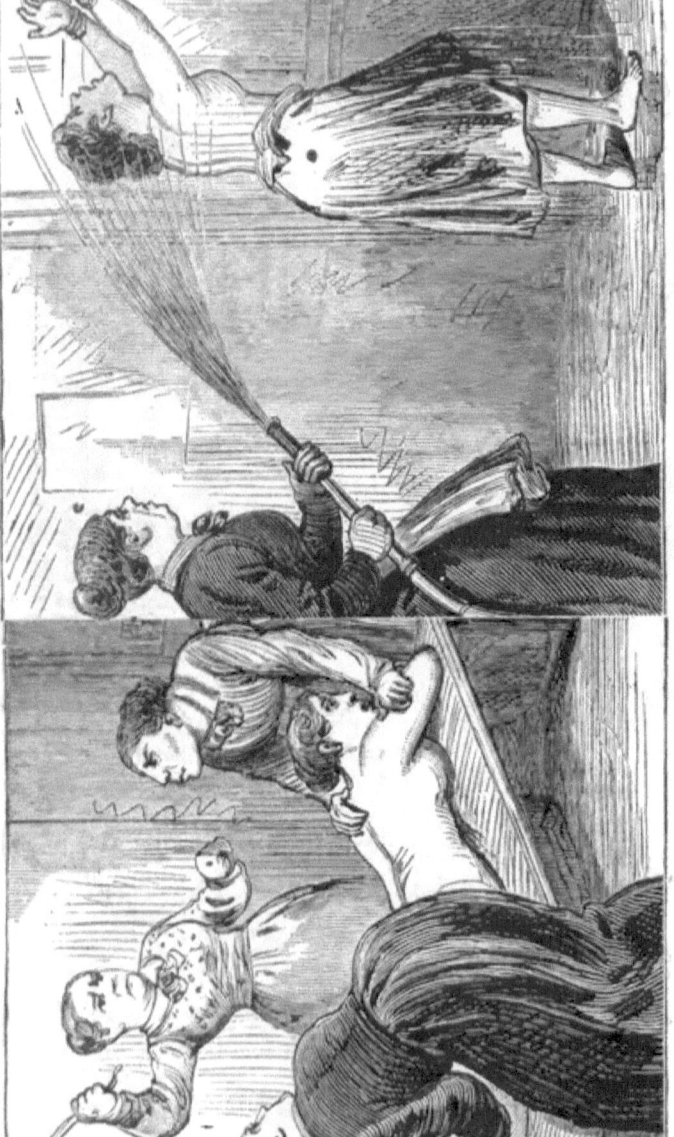

TORTURING AN APOSTATE.

mother and grandmother along with the daughter. **Literally in Utah men frequently marry a whole family.** A wife getting old is often glad to have her husband marry her daughter by another husband, so that the original wife may not be ousted from her **privileges and a comfortable home.**

It is a custom in Utah to call a woman after her husband's first name, in order to distinguish her. For instance, the wife of John Young is called Libbie John, and not Mrs. John Young. Brigham had only two sons by his first wife, Brigham and this John, the youngest. No fairy prince in the "Arabian Nights" was ever handsomer than John. He was the one who went East, renounced Mormonism, and divorced two wives for the sake of marrying the daughter of a Philadelphia physician.

Up to a certain point the history of John and Libbie is well known; how she separated from him when, violating his promise to have no wife but her, he married again. As she is still his wife, he supports her, she going backward and forward between the States and the Territory to meet him. She has obtained a great deal of praise for her spirited action in leaving him, and sympathy for her grief; but she is only suffering what his other wives suffered, and as he divorced them for her sake, what fealty could she have expected from such a man.

I remember one day sitting with a lady, when a neighbor rushed in breathless with a piece of news. "Oh, Mrs. S——!" she exclaimed, "do you know your husband is married to Mollie ——?"

"Indeed!" said my friend.

"Yes, and what's more, he has been married to her for some time."

"Well," replied the wife, "I hope he treats her like a lady, for she is a very nice girl."

The news was premature, for the husband was only paying attention to her, and having obtained the first wife's consent, he married her. They lived like two sisters. The man owned a small farm, and one day he had a paralytic stroke, and could no longer take care of it, so the women managed it and took care of him, and when he died it was divided equally between them. "Now, how much nicer this is," said the widows, "than to have let the property go out of the family because we could not get along together!"

The readiness with which some Mormon women acquiesce in the setting up of a rival to them in their husbands' affections is explicable upon the ground of superstition alone. The really devoted Mormons believe that those who do not practice polygamy are wrong, and not they; and they, especially the women, are fond of inveighing against the immorality of the States—the flirtation and worse of Gentile wives, and the unfaithfulness of Gentile husbands.

One part of their religion speciously appeals to the superstitious, credulous element in woman's nature. It is that no woman can enter the kingdom of heaven unless as the wife of some man; hence old maids are scarce in Utah. If a woman is resolutely opposed to matrimony and especially polygamy, sealing overcomes the difficulty. Sealing constitutes a nominal marriage, and also helps a woman financially, for a husband is bound to do something for every one of his sealed wives, if it is but to send her a pound of tea weekly. I know three old maids—the oldest is about 80. They weave rag carpets for a living, and are all sealed to the same man, who furnish their groceries and insures their entrance into heaven. If an old maid has neglected to be sealed, and she is on her death bed, some neighbor will be hurriedly sent for to be sealed to her. The ceremony is simple, consisting of a few words and a little anointing with oil.

Neither falsehood or concealment is necessary to a Mormon in making his plural union. Number one is taken into his confidence from the beginning, and her consent respectfully requested to every subsequent marriage is a formality never dispensed with. Until she is too old to hold her own at all, she is the head and ruler of the bevy of wives. Every wife is given so much and no more of the husband's time and money, thus preventing jealousy and dispute. He spends a week with one, a week with another, or less time if his wives be many. If he takes a fancy to remain longer than the allotted time woe be to him, for all the other wives rise up as one united injured woman, and make it lively for him. You see, it may not always be practicable for one wife to make a husband toe the mark, but a dozen, more or less, find it no trouble whatever.

One singular thing in Mormon families is the perfect good feeling which invariably exist among the children. They never quarrel, as step-sisters and brothers do in the States, for they are early taught that their rights are equal and respect them, their common father taking care to show no more favoritism among his children than among his wives. I was often amused at these same Mormon children. They would come in and say, "Mother, Polly So-and-so is going to be married to Mr. What's-his-name. She's going in fifth, or ninth, or eleventh," as the case might be. And then mother and children would sit and discuss the news as a Christian family would talk about a wedding next door.

CHAPTER XII.

MEN WITH MANY WIVES.

I have alluded to the wife who obtained a divorce from Brigham Young, Ann Eliza. She was a thorough Mormon, ambitious and intriguing for power. She wanted the glory of being one of Brigham's wives, and divorced a husband in order to reign supreme over his vast estates and many wives. Brigham, however, was enamored of Amelia, and was wooing her. Now the Mormon women have a sort of confessional, in the sacred precincts of which they may safely confide their desire to marry a certain man, who is thereupon informed of the wish by the pious go-between, and the gentleman can hardly refuse. Ann Eliza would not take no for an answer—and no Brigham did say to her, I know for a certainty—so she became the nineteenth wife. He made Eliza's honeymoon as brief as possible, and hurried to Amelia again.

Eliza, like all the rest of his wives, was given a choice of residence. She selected a pretty little well-stocked farm about four miles from Salt Lake City. She struggled hard for the office of queen bee, but there is no such sinecure. She was so nettled at Brigham's infrequent and quite ceremonious calls that she took a dislike to her farm, and thought that if she were to get within the city limits she would get more chance at him, so she teased and tortured him until he gave her a house in town. It was a very comfortable, commodious dwelling, very roomy, and well adapted for a boarding house.

By this time the Gentiles had overrun the Mormon fastnesses, and where the American goes there the boarding house follows. The nineteenth wife could not become the power behind the throne, so she resolved to open a boarding house. Brigham thought it beneath the dignity of his wife, infinitesimally speaking, to keep a boarding house, but she pestered him so he consented. He had married her to get rid of her, and, not succeeding, he thought the boarding house would quiet her. She took in some Gentiles who backed her in open rebellion, wrote her lecture, and started her lecturing. This was the inner life of Brigham and Eliza.

Amelia Folsom, her successful rival, was the closest approach to a boss Brigham Young ever had. She is a native of Portsmouth, New Hampshire. She is tall, well formed, with light hair and gray eyes, and regular features, and has but little refinement of manner. When at the theatre sitting in the king's box with her husband, the observed of all observers, she may be seen eating apples, throwing the skins about, chatting with Brigham, and occasionally leveling her glass at some one in the assembly. She plays and sings with indifferent skill and taste. She was for a long time unwilling to marry the President, but he was really dead in love with her and continued his suit till by repeated promises of advancement made to herself and her parents he finally succeeded. For several months he urged his suit, during which time his carriage might be seen almost any day standing at her father's door, for hours at a time.

When he got her he discovered that he had caught a tartar. She was jealous, fierce and cross-grained, and led him a sorry life in private. She was tyrannical, and ruled the women of the harem with a strong hand. Poor Emmeline, who next preceded Amelia as the favorite, was quite broken-hearted. In fact, all the women were unhappy and miserable. A common remark in reply to the usual salutation was, "Oh, I've got the blues to-day," and they never got out of them till death broke the family up and sent Amelia off into retirement.

Brigham had near his house two additional houses, one where his wives and their children lived, and adjoining it a storehouse, where groceries, clothing and other necessities were dispensed. One afternoon Brigham was sitting on his stoop, next to Cannon's newspaper office, talking to Bishop Welles, his principal aide-de-camp, when a little girl of about seven years approached him and said:

"Please, papa, can I hab a pair ov soo's?"

"Shoes, eh?" answered Brigham.

A WHOLESALE MORMON.

MADE GOOD USE OF HIS WIVES.

"Yeth, thir!" said the little one.

"Well, who's your mamma?" asked Brigham.

"My mamma!" answered the child.

"Yes, yes, I know; but what's her name?" inquired Brigham.

"I guess it's Ellen's child," said Bishop Welles.

"Oh, yes; I believe it is!" said Brigham. Then turning to the child he wrote an order:

"Give Sister Ellen's child a pair of shoes, and charge to her account.   B. Y."

It is not uncommon for a woman, who is the lawful wife of a Gentile, to leave her husband and live as a wife of a Mormon. Brigham Young had a woman in his harem who was the wife of a gentleman in Boston, and Parley Pratt, once one of the most prominent apostles, was shot and killed by an enraged husband for taking his wife from California to Salt Lake City, and there marrying her.

Divorces are granted by the First President. I knew a woman in Salt Lake City who had been married six times, and all her husbands were living.

The tendency of polygamy being to immorality generally, I might refer to indecency in conversation as particularly observed. This occurs with women and children as well as men. Several wives of one man, with their children present, have been known to indulge in such indecent conversation as would bring the blush to the face of a modest woman if repeated to her alone. The result of this may be seen in the precociousness of their children in certain ways. Urchins of eight or nine know more of what they should not know than youths of sixteen or eighteen in a refined community. They are not only afforded opportunities of thus corrupting their minds, but often encouraged to do so.

Recently a boy of 16, the leader of a band of highwaymen, after the perpetration of an atrocious murder, was caught and lynched. From his childhood the boy was conspicuous for cruelty. Every living thing that approached him, if it was weaker than he was, suffered. A well-known Mormon Bishop condoled with the mother, one of the wives of a leading Mormon. "Do not insult me with your condolence," the poor woman exclaimed. "It was the poor boy's misfortune, not his fault. Mormonism is alone to blame. My husband came here to do business. As soon as he began to grow rich he was told that Mormon patronage would be withdrawn unless he became a Mormon and took a second wife. We had been very happy together, but my husband was tempted by the hope of becoming rich, and he agreed to take a second wife. She was 'sealed' to him in the Endowment House, and duly installed in our home. I was almost maddened, and, before my boy's birth, I had no other thought,than the killing of the woman who had supplanted me. That evil thought marked him for a murderer, and he is what your church's crime and his father's folly made him."

I accompanied my husband recently on a surveying expedition. At about sundown one afternoon when we were on the outskirts of a small settlement a part of the harness on one of our horses broke. We went to the nearest house to get a tool to repair the harness. In a room about 18 feet square I saw a rough-looking man, three women and a number of children, ranging from infants almost to young men and women. I found that the women were the man's wives and the mothers of the children. They bore the relations to each other of grandmother, mother and daughter.

Is it any wonder that Heber C. Kimball used to call the disgraces to their sex who will submit to such a system as this his "cows?"

A young girl of Mormonistic parentage observed even noticing a Gentile is called to a very strict account. A good story is told of Bret Harte in this connection, which is well worth repeating.

Some twelve years ago Bret was visiting there in company with Sam Ralston, of San Francisco, and after playing a game of billiards strolled down the street, intending to visit the theatre and see Lotta, who was playing that evening. As they came near the theatre Ralston noticed two young ladies who had come up in the stage with them from Ogden and with whom they had kept up quite a flirtation. Nudging Bret he raised his hat and said:

"Good evening, ladies, going to see Lotta?" The young ladies looked at them a minute, when the elder of the two said:

"You will be arrested if you don't look out."

Bret Harte, thinking something in the action of Ralston or himself had offended them, said:

"Is it customary here to arrest gentlemen because they politely speak to ladies?"

"No," said the young lady, "not because they speak to ladies but because they are Gentiles and dare address Joseph Smith's chosen people."

"Well, then, I'll see Joe; where is he?" inquired Bret, not at all abashed.

"Sir," said the lady, "there's my father, ask him."

Bret politely bowed to the old hayseed gatherer and said:

"Your daughter informs me that you are one of Joe Smith's people. I once knew a Joe Smith at Petoluma, who was one of the best poker players on the flat, only he lost his ear ringing in a cold deck on Tom—"

"Say," broke in the father, "say, young man, I doan't know yer and I doan't want ter. Joseph Smith, sah, is our Saviour, the same as yours and—"

"Well, sir, you'll excuse me, I'm sure," exclaimed Bret, "but I'm d—d if I want to meet your Saviour if he don't save you folks any better than he seems to."

And grabbing Ralston's arm the author of the "Heathen Chinee" made a break for the nearest bar-room.

CHAPTER XIII.

A MORMON WIFE'S STORY.

The following story of the life of a friend of mine, a victim of the accursed system of polygamy, will be found interesting in its very simplicity. It tells in the plainest language a romance no pen of fiction could equal in grim, blood-curdling eloquence of facts.

This is the story.

I was born and raised in New York city. When seventeen years of age a severe attack of lung fever struck me down, so that my life was despaired of. While lying in this condition a young man who formerly worked for my father, but two years before my attack had gone to Utah, returned to New York and advised me to send for a Mormon elder, who, he declared, could cure me by the laying on of hands. My parents were Methodists and considered the advice as an insult, but in my weak and despairing frame of mind I told the young man to bring the Mormon elder. When the elder came he laid his two hands on my forehead. Immediately I felt three rigors pass from my head to feet and five minutes afterward I felt entirely recovered.

Firmly impressed that a miracle had been worked on me I felt that the elder was a man of God and I embraced Mormonism, being baptized one week after in the river at the foot of Canal street. A few months after this I was married to William Hunt and together we settled down in New York. We lived very happily together. In the spring of 1862 the Church Elders wanted us to remove to the land of Zion. I talked with Mr. Hunt about it; told him I had heard that men there practiced polygamy and I thought we had better not go. He coincided with me, but the heads of the church said it was our duty to go, and my husband and I soon consented.

We went overland to Salt Lake City and began life in that place. Children were born to us until we had seven and they were our delight. We prospered in everything that increased our boundless wealth of happiness. But one day there came a change. William came home and said that Brigham had ordered him to take another wife.

I almost fainted when he told me this and William declared to me that he would not go into polygamy.

But I had misgivings and these harassed me by day and night. I had a servant girl living with me, who came West with us, and as she was so good to the children I thought a great deal of her. She was young and I had almost a mother's feeling for her.

William came again to me one day and said that he was endangering his hope for salvation by refusing to go into polygamy. The Church teaches that no man can reach the highest happiness hereafter, unless he shall have had a plurality of wives. Well, I begged him as only a loving wife about to lose her idol can, on my knees I implored him to leave Utah; to think of our children, of our love and of the many days of undisturbed happiness. But he argued with me by saying that he should obey the ordinance of God; that if he took another wife it would not change his old love, that I would always be first in his heart.

Up to this time I did not suspect whom William was expecting to marry, but at length when he told me he was about to be sealed to Jane, my servant girl, I went to her and pleaded with her to give up the idea. She seemed to feel bad but still declared her love for him. I did not know what to do. I felt murder in my heart and could have

TOO MUCH MOTHER-IN-LAW.

THE ATONEMENT OF BLOOD.

killed both my husband and Jane, but still I loved him with the wildest infatuation.

At length the day came for the wedding and I was asked if I desired to witness the marriage ceremony. I said "Yes" and went to the Endowment House with my brain on fire and so overcome that I fainted three times in the building before the marriage ceremony was completed. Just before sealing the two Brigham Young turned to me and asked:

"Sister Hunt, do you consent to the marriage of your husband to this woman?"

I replied: "Yes and No."

"This is a very singular answer. What do you mean, sister?"

"I mean that if this is the only way my husband can see God and attain a blessed life everlasting, then yes; but speaking from my heart and with a wife's world of love, I reply no, no, a thousand times; for his life eternal, I can say yes, but if it is my life that depends upon this issue, I say no; I would rather abide in hell than have him marry another woman."

This answer was regarded as a consent and my husband received a second wife, while my heart perished forever when they were pronounced one.

But the loss of my husband in this manner was but the beginning of a system of persecution, to which I was a victim for two years. Mr. Hunt had no sooner taken his new and young wife home than he began to despise me. The girl too, a wife jointly with me, turned against me. One week after the marriage, as we were walking together, I asked Jane why she treated me so coldly. She replied:

"It is because I hate you, and I hate you because you are the wife of Mr. Hunt."

This new wife of William's adopted a new life; instead of working as before marriage, she assumed the mistresship, and I had to perform all the labor that was not done by my children. Daily I was the enforced witness of their love-making—the new wife on the knee and in the embrace of my husband. I was not allowed any privileges, and my children were thrust aside by their father and Jane. We had frequent brawls, and many times my husband has struck me down with his fist. At length my burden of trouble had become so great that I resolved to commit suicide.

In pursuance of this resolve I went to a drug store and purchased twenty-five cents worth of laudanum. The druggist seemed to suspect my motives, for he asked me what I wanted the drug for. I replied that it was for a sore throat. He then insisted on mixing some tincture of myrrh with it, and then, taking the bottle, I went into a sunflower patch and drank the contents. When I realized my deed, I knelt down and poured my soul out in prayer for forgiveness. I then went home, and as I reached the door my youngest little girl came running toward me crying, and said:

"Oh, mamma, I'se so dad you tome; papa won't dive me any dinna and I'se so hungy."

I saw Mr. Hunt and his wife sitting at the table eating by themselves, while my children were driven into the garden. My God! said I, what have I done! What a coward I have been to kill myself and leave these children without one to love them. I had not been in the house more than five minutes when I began to feel the effects of the laudanum. I asked Jane if she would be a mother to my children if I died.

"No, never; I will have nothing to do with your brats," she replied.

I then more fully realized the enormity of my crime, and I prayed that my life might be spared for my children's sake. But the deadly drug began to do its work; my head was bursting, my eyes were turning inward, while my ears were assailed with the most deafening noises, cannons firing, drums beating, fiends shouting, water roaring, and a confusion of noises which tore my brain as with re-hot pincers. Still I was conscious. I could still hear Jane crying:

"Oh, she is dying; go for the Elder!"

But my husband only cursed me and said, "I hope she will die."

He demanded of me to know what I had taken, but I refused to tell him. When I became unconscious at last, they found the empty bottle in my pocket, and then I was put to bed by Jane (my husband cursing me all the time). I drank two teacupfuls of soft soap grease, which proved an emetic that saved my life.

When I recovered my husband continually upbraided me on my unsuccessful attempt at suicide, saying he wished I would complete the job, and so exasperated me that at length I again resolved to do

AT LAST THE BODY SAT UP.

SHE DESCENDED FROM THE TABLE WITH HER GRAVE CLOTHES ON.

the deed; but when about to execute the act a voice sounded in my ear, saying, "Wait."

I did not understand the warning, but obeyed.

That warning saved me from a suicide's grave. It gave me strength to live for my children, and I have borne it all. Two years ago my husband rented a house for himself and Jane, and I have never lived with them since. Jane, three weeks after giving birth to a child, left him, and he is now a drunkard on the streets of Salt Lake City, an object of pity. I have no further feeling but pity for him, for God has made him suffer, and time makes all things even. Twice have attempts been made on my life by the Danites for revealing the secrets of polygamy, but a higher power has sustained me. No human being ever suffered more than I. May God give me recompense!

This story I have necessarily summarized, but it is bad enough, and yet it is a story that will describe the lives of nearly every polygamist's wife.

CHAPTER XIV.

THE DOOM OF MORMONISM.

Since the death of Brigham Young there has been a great change in the church government. During his life everything appertaining to the sect was tributary to him, especially the revenue. Now, however, the financial government is entrusted to four elders of the church. John Taylor, president of the church and successor to Brigham Young, has accomplished a reorganization and now confines the duties of president to theological management, leaving the commerce to business men. Taylor is a very clever old man, nearly eighty years of age, and always makes a good impression on those who visit him. Last year he took another wife in the person of a widow named Barrett. This lady is a native of England and became a convert several years ago. She came to Utah with five hundred other proselytes and brought with her $750,000, which she realized from the sale of her estates in England. This large sum of money was a morsel after which Brigham thirsted mightily and he courted the widow by day and night, inside and outside the Temple; but she wouldn't wed him because there came to her ears many stories concerning the ill-treatment of women in the presidential harem. Taylor, however, conducted a more successful siege, for, after battering the widow's ramparts for one year, she capitulated and the twain are now nine—the president having had seven wives before he took Mrs. Barrett.

The church is now in a flourishing condition, with a tithing collection of $1,000,000 annually and an increase of from fifteen hundred to twenty-five hundred annually in church membership. Idaho and Montana are peopling rapidly with Latter Day Saints, too.

* * * * * * * *

John Taylor, who is an Englishman as I have already said, succeeded to Brigham Young's office in 1877. But the man who really rules the 120,000 Mormons in Utah is George L. Cannon. Cannon is an Englishman, too, has sat in Congress as territorial delegate from Utah and is the Mormon attorney at Washington. He is a shrewd and able man, who with the same opportunity would more than rival Brigham Young as a leader.

But his opportunity is gone.

The opening of the Pacific road has been the first step toward the overthrow of Mormonism. The Latter Day Saints no longer live intrenched beyond the reach of the government whose laws they violate, but are surrounded by settlements and within easy reach of an army.

It was a part of the policy of the late President Garfield to open an active campaign against the Mormon infamy and his successor has adopted the same purpose. President Arthur in his inaugural message painted Mormonism out as an evil calling loudly for reform and in the present state of popular opinion in regard to it it cannot be very long before it is taken sternly in hand.

How soon that will be it is difficult to prophecy, but the black outrage of Mormonism cannot continue unmolested many years longer. The people are awakening and crying out for justice against it, and when the American people wake and cry for justice they generally get it.

That the Mormons will offer any active resistance to Government interference with their loathsome practices it is difficult to believe. Their fanaticism is savage, but their leaders have brains and it is scarcely probably that they would invite utter ruin by violence, when by submitting to authority they know must eventually overpower them they can save their hoarded wealth at the expense of a sovereignty they cannot continue to wield for another generation.

In a recent article on this subject an able writer entitled his essay "The Mormon at Bay."

That term exactly specifies the present condition of the foul creed founded by Joe Smith and Sidney Rigdon.

It is at bay, like some obscene monster which the hunters have encompassed. Civilization has surrounded it and is closing in upon it. The hands of all decent men are raised against it and it can only await its deathblow with what philosophy it may command.

When it is hurled to ruin there will fall the most monstrous structure of fraud and infamy cemented by the blood of sacrifice ever reared in the history of the world and a creed of lust that transforms a vast stretch of our continent into a community of prostitution, and physical and mental debasement will become the by-word for iniquity it is still a triumphant monument to.

THE END.

www.ingramcontent.com/pod-product-compliance
Lightning Source LLC
Chambersburg PA
CBHW020158170426
43199CB00010B/1100